Computer Basics

PEARSON

Prentice
Hall

Harlow, England • London • New York • Boston • San Francisco • Toronto • Sydney • Singapore • Hong Kong
Tokyo • Seoul • Taipei • New Delhi • Cape Town • Madrid • Mexico City • Amsterdam • Munich • Paris • Milan

PEARSON EDUCATION LIMITED

Edinburgh Gate
Harlow CM20 2JE
Tel: +44 (0)1279 623623
Fax: +44 (0)1279 431059
Website: www.pearsoned.co.uk

First published in Great Britain in 2009

© Joli Ballew 2009

ISBN: 978–0–273–72347–9

British Library Cataloguing-in-Publication Data
A catalogue record for this book is available from the British Library

Library of Congress Cataloging-in-Publication Data
Ballew, Joli.
  Computer basics in simple steps / Joli Ballew.--1st ed.
      p. cm.
  ISBN 978-0-273-72347-9 (pbk.)
  1. Computers. I. Title.
  QA76.5.B26213 2009
  004--dc22
                    2009009527

10 9 8 7 6 5 4 3 2 1
13 12 11 10 09

Designed by pentacorbig, High Wycombe

Typeset in 11/14 pt ITC Stone Sans by 30
Printed and bound in Great Britain by Ashford Colour Press Ltd, Gosport, Hants

The publisher's policy is to use paper manufactured from sustainable forests.

Computer Basics

in Simple steps

Joli Ballew

Use your computer with confidence

Get to grips with practical computing tasks with minimal time, fuss and bother.

In Simple Steps guides guarantee immediate results. They tell you everything you need to know on a specific application; from the most essential tasks to master, to every activity you'll want to accomplish, through to solving the most common problems you'll encounter.

Helpful features

To build your confidence and help you to get the most out of your computer, practical hints, tips and shortcuts feature on every page:

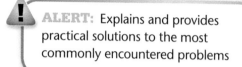 **ALERT:** Explains and provides practical solutions to the most commonly encountered problems

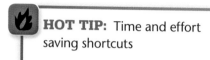 **HOT TIP:** Time and effort saving shortcuts

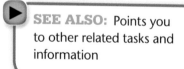 **SEE ALSO:** Points you to other related tasks and information

 **DID YOU KNOW?** Additional features to explore

WHAT DOES THIS MEAN?
Jargon and technical terms explained in plain English

Practical. Simple. Fast.

in Simple steps

Dedication:

For Mom and Papa John, may you both rest in peace.

Author acknowledgments:

I just love writing for Pearson Education, and these *In Simple Steps* books prove it. Three books in almost as many months! It's wonderful working with Steve Temblett, Laura Blake and the rest of the gang. It's not often I find a team that works so well together.

I'd also like to acknowledge my agent, Neil Salkind, who works hard for me always, and my family, Dad, Jennifer, and Cosmo. I wish my mom could be here to see these books; she would have enjoyed them. You may see her in a few of the pictures here.

Contents at a glance

Contents

1 Set up a PC or laptop

2 First steps

3 Common tasks

9 Stay secure

10 Digital pictures

11 Music, DVDs and Windows Media Player

12 Change system defaults

13 Share data and printers

14 Use Help and Support

15 Improve computer performance

16 Fix problems

Top 10 Computer Basics Problems Solved

Top 10 Computer Basics Tips

Tip 1: Set up a PC

To set up a new PC you need to connect all of the appropriate pieces, including the power cable, monitor, keyboard and mouse.

1. Locate the power cord. It may consist of two pieces that need to be connected.

2. Connect the power cord to the back of the PC or the side of the laptop, as noted in the documentation. You may see a symbol similar to the one shown here.

3. Plug the power cord into the wall outlet.

4. Place the monitor where desired, but within reach of the computer's tower.

5. Plug in the monitor to a wall outlet so that it has power.

6. Locate the cord that connects the monitor to the PC and look at the end of the cord.

7. Find the compatible connection on the PC tower.

8. Make the connection.

9. Connect the mouse to an available USB port. It will only fit one way.

10. Repeat to connect the USB keyboard.

Tip 2: Write a letter

You can use Notepad to type a quick memo, note or letter. You can access Notepad from the Start menu.

1 Click Start.

2 In the Start Search window, type Notepad.

3 Click Notepad under Programs. (Note that you may see other results, as shown here.)

4 Click once inside Notepad, and start typing.

5 When you have written your letter, you can either save it or print it from the File menu. Click File.

6 Click Save.

7 Type a name for the file.

8 Click Save.

9 Click File.

10 Click Print.

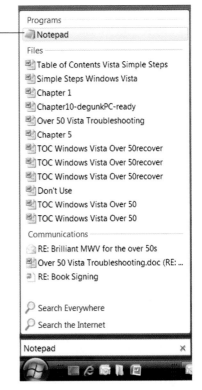

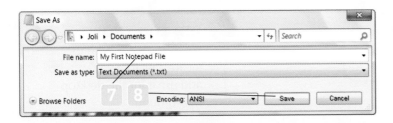

Tip 3: Change the background and screen saver

One of the first things you may like to do when you get a new PC or upgrade an older one is to personalise the picture on the Desktop. That picture is called the background.

1 Right-click an empty area of the Desktop.

2 Click Personalize.

3 Click Desktop Background.

4 For Location, select Windows Wallpapers. If it is not chosen already, click the down arrow to locate it.

5 Use the scroll bars to locate the wallpaper to use as your Desktop background.

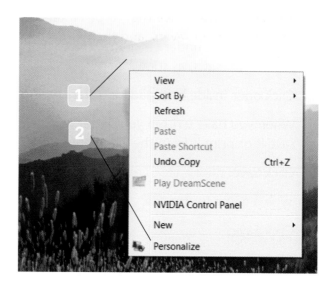

Personalize appearance and sounds

Window Color and Appearance
Fine tune the color and style of your windows.

Desktop Background ——— 3
Choose from available backgrounds or colors or use one of your own pictures to decorate the desktop.

Screen Saver
Change your screen saver or adjust when it displays. A screen saver is a picture or animation that covers your screen and appears when your computer is idle for a set period of time.

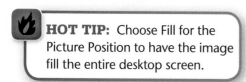 **HOT TIP:** Choose Fill for the Picture Position to have the image fill the entire desktop screen.

 **DID YOU KNOW?**
You can click Browse to locate a picture you've taken and use it for the desktop background.

6 Select a background to use.

7 Select a positioning option (the default is the most common).

8 Click OK.

9 Click Screen Saver.

10 Click the arrow to see the available screen savers, and then select one.

11 Use the arrows to change how long to wait before the screen saver is enabled.

12 If desired, click On resume, display logon screen to require a password to log back into the computer.

13 Click OK.

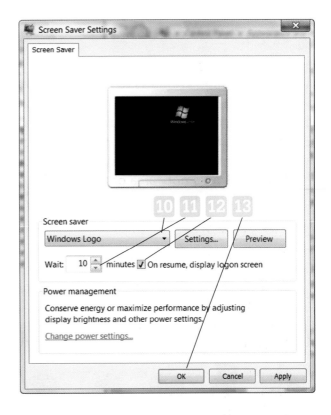

 HOT TIP: If you keep a lot of icons on your desktop, consider a solid colour. It will be less distracting when trying to find an icon.

Tip 4: Play a game

Windows Vista and Windows XP both come with lots of games. You access the available games from the Games folder on the Start menu. (In XP, click Start and then All Programs to access the Games folder.) Each game offers instructions for how to play it. For the most part, moving a player, tile or card, dealing a card, or otherwise moving around the screen is performed using the mouse or arrow keys.

1 Click Start.

2 Click Games.

3 Double-click any game to begin the game.

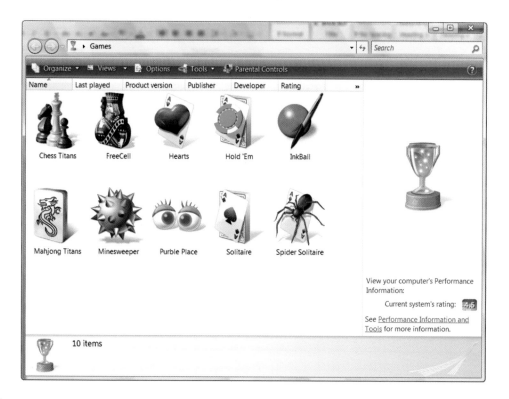

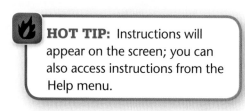

HOT TIP: Instructions will appear on the screen; you can also access instructions from the Help menu.

Tip 5: Compose and send an email

You compose an email message by clicking Create Mail on the Windows Mail toolbar after your email account has been configured. You input who the email should be sent to, and the subject, and then you type the message.

1 Click Create Mail.

2 Type the recipient's email address in the To line. If you want to add additional names, separate each email address with a semicolon.

3 Type a subject in the Subject field.

4 Type the message in the body pane.

5 Click Send.

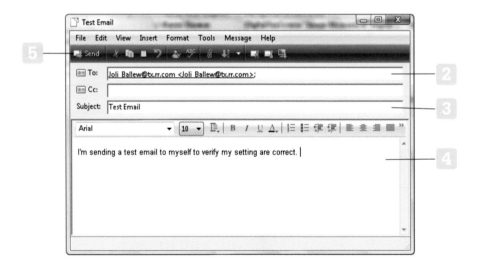

? **DID YOU KNOW?**

If you want to send the email to someone and you don't need them to respond, you can put them in the CC line.

Tip 6: Access a website

Windows Vista comes with Internet Explorer, an application you can use to surf the Internet. Internet Explorer is a Web browser, and it has everything you need, including an application to block annoying pop-ups and the ability to save your favourite webpages. You'll use Internet Explorer to surf the Internet.

1 Open Internet Explorer. A website will probably open automatically.

2 To open a new website, drag your mouse across the website name to select it. Do not drag your mouse over the http://www part of the address.

3 Type the name of the website you'd like to visit in the address bar. Try http://www.amazon .com.

HOT TIP: You can open Internet Explorer from the Start menu or Quick Launch toolbar; just look for the blue E.

WHAT DOES THIS MEAN?

Address bar: used to type in Internet addresses, also known as URLs (uniform resource locators). Generally, an Internet address takes the form of http://www.companyname.com.

4 Press Enter on the keyboard.

ALERT: Websites almost always start with http://www.

? DID YOU KNOW?

.com is the most popular website ending; it means that the website is a company, business or personal website. .edu is used for educational institutions, .gov for government entities, .org is mostly used for non-profit organisations, and .net for miscellaneous businesses, companies and personal websites. There are also others, such as .info, .biz, .tv and .uk.com.

Tip 7: Back up a folder to an external drive

You can copy the folders to an external drive to create a back-up. You copy the folder to the external drive in the same way that you'd copy a folder to another area of your hard drive: you open both folders and then drag and drop.

1 Click Start and click Computer.

2 Locate the external drive. (Leave this window open and resize it so that it takes up only part of the screen.)

3 Locate a folder (or folders) to copy. Resize this window as shown here, so that you can drag and drop between the two open windows.

4 Position the windows so you can see them both.

5 Right-click the folder to copy.

6 While holding down the right mouse key, drag the folder to the new location.

7 Drop it there.

8 Choose Copy Here.

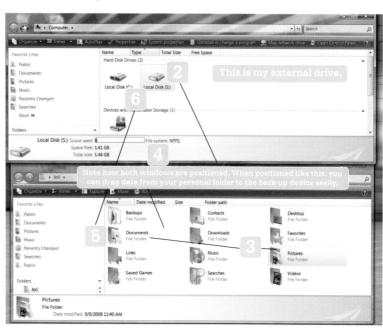

This is my external drive.

Note how both windows are positioned. When positioned like this, you can drag data from your personal folder to the back-up device easily.

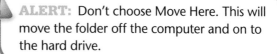

▶ **SEE ALSO:** Restoring and moving a window are covered in Chapter 6.

HOT TIP: Click Start and click your personal folder (the one with your name on it) to locate a folder to copy.

⚠ **ALERT:** Don't choose Move Here. This will move the folder off the computer and on to the hard drive.

Tip 8: Upload a digital picture from a digital camera, phone or memory card

After you've taken pictures with your digital camera or mobile phone, you'll want to move or copy those pictures to the computer. Once stored on the computer's hard drive, you can view, edit, email and print the pictures, among other things.

1. Connect the device. If applicable, turn it on. If the device uses a memory card and you have a memory card slot, you can insert the card into the slot instead of connecting the device.

2. When prompted, choose Import Pictures using Windows.

3. Type a descriptive name for the group of pictures you're importing.

4. Click Import.

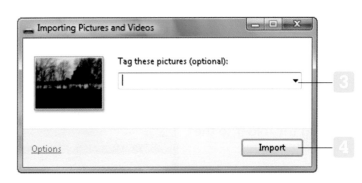

 ALERT: Before you can upload pictures from a digital camera, you must install the camera.

HOT TIP: If desired, tick Erase after importing. This will cause Vista to erase the images from the device after the import is complete.

Tip 9: Copy a CD to your hard drive

You can copy music CDs to your hard drive. This is called 'ripping'. Once music is on your computer, you can listen to it in Media Player, burn compilations of music to other CDs and put the music on a portable music player.

1   Insert the CD to copy into the CD drive.

2   If any pop-up boxes appear, click the X to close them.

3   In Windows Media Player, click the Rip button.

4   Deselect any songs you do not want to copy to your computer.

5   Click Start Rip.

Help and Support is located on the Start menu.

 Click Start.

 Click Help and Support.

 Click any item in Help and Support to 'drill down' into the help topics.

 You can also click Options and Browse Help, or choose to view a Table of Contents.

? DID YOU KNOW?

Pressing F1 almost always opens the help pages for the open application. If no application is open, it opens Windows Help and Support.

1 Set up a PC or laptop

Introduction

New PCs and laptops come with instructions for setting them up. If you have instructions, you should follow them. However, if you purchased a used computer or one was handed down to you, you probably won't have anything to guide you through the process. If that's the case, you can follow the instructions here. Once you've connected the monitor, mouse, keyboard, and speakers, you can then concentrate on connecting and installing non-essential items like a printer, webcam, and other hardware.

Locate and plug in the power cable

The power cable is the cable that you will use to connect your computer to the wall outlet (power outlet). Sometimes a power cord has two parts that need to be connected.

1 Locate the power cord. It may consist of two pieces that need to be connected.

2 Connect the power cord to the back or side of the computer, as noted in the documentation. You may see a symbol similar to the one shown here.

3 Plug the power cord into the wall outlet.

? DID YOU KNOW?

When you connect the power cable for a laptop, the laptop will use the power from the outlet and charge the battery at the same time. When you unplug the laptop from the power outlet, the laptop will run on stored battery power.

HOT TIP: Purchase and place a surge protector between the PC and the wall outlet. This will protect the PC from power surges that could damage it.

Connect the monitor

Your PC comes with a monitor that has to be connected. Older PCs use a connection like the one shown here, but newer PCs can have different types of connection.

1 Place the monitor where desired, but within reach of the computer's tower.

2 Plug in the monitor to a wall outlet so that it has power.

3 Locate the cord that connects the monitor to the PC and look at the end of the cord.

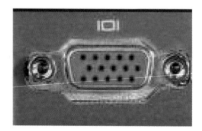

4 Find the compatible connection on the PC tower.

5 Make the connection.

WHAT DOES THIS MEAN?

DVI port: Used to connect the computer to a television set or other DVI device.

S-Video: Used to connect the computer to a television or other display that also offers s-video connectivity.

 HOT TIP: Don't turn on the monitor yet. Wait until you turn on the PC, and then turn on the monitor.

 HOT TIP: Most monitor connections plug in to a compatible port on the tower and also have two screws for securing the connection.

Connect a USB mouse and keyboard

USB (universal serial bus) ports offer a place to connect USB devices. USB devices include mice, external keyboards and other devices.

1 Connect the mouse to an available USB port. It will only fit one way.

2 Repeat to connect the USB keyboard.

 ALERT: If you have an older PC, you may have a keyboard and mouse that do not connect via USB. If that's the case, match the connector to the appropriate port on the back of the PC to install it.

HOT TIP: Here's what USB ports look like on a laptop. You may want to connect an external mouse here.

Connect external speakers or headphones

If there are any external sound ports, you'll probably see three. Most of the time you have access to a line-in jack, a microphone-in jack and a headphones/speaker/line-out jack.

> ## WHAT DOES THIS MEAN?
>
> **Line-in jack**: Accepts audio from external devices, such as CD players.
>
> **Microphone-in jack**: Accepts input from external microphones.
>
> **Headphone or speaker jack**: Lets you connect your PC to an external source for output, including, but not limited to, speakers and headphones.

1 If necessary, plug the device into an electrical outlet.

2 If necessary, turn on the speakers.

3 Insert the cables that connect to the device to the computer, using the proper port.

4 If prompted, work through any set-up processes.

? DID YOU KNOW?

Line-in jacks bring data into the computer; line-out jacks port data out to external devices such as speakers and headphones.

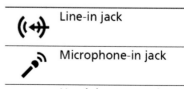

Line-in jack

Microphone-in jack

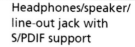

Headphones/speaker/line-out jack with S/PDIF support

Connect and install a printer

Most of the time, to install a printer you insert the CD that came with the printer, plug in the printer, turn it on, and wait for Windows XP or Windows Vista to install it automatically. However, it's always best to have directions for performing a task, so in that vein I've included them here.

 ALERT: It's usually best to connect the new printer, turn it on and let the operating system (OS) install it. You need to intervene only when the OS can't install the printer on its own.

ALERT: Read the directions that come with each new device that you acquire. If there are specific instructions for installing the driver, follow those directions rather than the generic directions offered here.

1 Connect the printer to a wall outlet.

2 Connect the printer to the PC using either a USB cable or a parallel port cable.

3 Insert the CD for the device, if you have it.

4 If a pop-up message appears regarding the CD, click the X to close the window.

5 Turn on the device.

6 Wait while the driver is installed. If you're using Windows Vista, you'll see what's shown here.

? DID YOU KNOW?
USB is a faster connection than a parallel port, but with a printer you probably won't notice the difference.

 ALERT: If the printer does not install properly, refer to the printer's user manual.

? DID YOU KNOW?
Leave the CD in the drive. If the computer wants any of the information on the CD, it will acquire it from there.

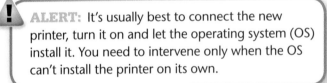

Connect and install a webcam

You install a webcam in the same way that you install a printer. You insert the CD that came with the webcam, plug it in and turn it on, and wait for the operating system to install it. However, it's always best to have directions for performing a task, so in that vein I've included them here.

1 Connect the camera to a wall outlet or insert fresh batteries.

2 Connect the camera to the PC using either a USB cable or a FireWire cable. Turn it on.

3 Insert the CD for the device, if you have it.

4 If a pop-up message appears regarding the CD, click the X to close the window.

5 Wait while the driver is installed.

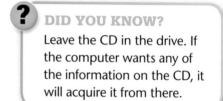

DID YOU KNOW?

Leave the CD in the drive. If the computer wants any of the information on the CD, it will acquire it from there.

DID YOU KNOW?

FireWire is faster than USB.

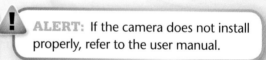

ALERT: If the camera does not install properly, refer to the user manual.

For a laptop: locate, insert or remove the battery

Laptops have batteries, but they don't come with the batteries installed. You have to install the battery yourself. The battery allows you to use the laptop when you're not connected to a power source. The battery must be charged before use.

1 If the computer is turned on, turn it off.

2 Unplug the laptop from the wall outlet and remove the power cable. Set the power cable aside.

3 Carefully turn the laptop upside-down and place it on a desk or table.

4 If applicable, locate the battery bay and open it.

5 If applicable, unlatch the battery latch.

6 Insert the battery.

7 Lock the battery into place.

8 Secure the latch.

9 If applicable, close the battery bay door.

WHAT DOES THIS MEAN?

Battery bay: This holds the computer's battery. Sometimes you have to use a screwdriver to get inside the battery bay; other times you simply need to slide out the compartment door.

Battery release latch: This holds the battery in place, even after the battery bay's door has been opened. You'll need to release this latch to get to the battery.

Battery lock: This locks the battery in position.

▶ **SEE ALSO:** Shutting down Windows safely is covered in Chapter 2.

? **DID YOU KNOW?**
Some batteries, like the one shown here, don't use a battery bay but simply click into place on the outside of the laptop.

Locate and press the power button

Before you can use your computer, you have to press the power button to start the operating system. The operating system is most likely Windows XP or Windows Vista and is what allows you to use the computer.

1 If applicable, open the laptop's lid.

2 Press the Start button to turn on the computer.

? DID YOU KNOW?
Starting a computer is also called 'booting' it.

! ALERT: It takes a minute or so for the computer to start. Be patient!

! ALERT: If you ever have trouble starting Windows Vista, during the boot-up process hit the F8 key on the keyboard. You can then choose from various startup options, such as safe mode.

? DID YOU KNOW?
Most of the time, the power button is at the top of the keyboard on a laptop or on the front of a PC tower for a desktop.

Connect additional hardware

For hardware other than printers and cameras, you'll need to insert a driver CD if one came with the hardware, plug in the new hardware and turn it on, and wait for the computer to install it.

1 Connect the hardware to the PC and/or a wall outlet.

Installing device driver software ×
Click here for status.

2:03 PM

2 Insert the CD for the device, if you have it.

3 If a pop-up message appears regarding the CD, click the X to close the window.

4 Turn on the device, if applicable.

5 Wait while the driver is installed.

WHAT DOES THIS MEAN?

Kensington lock slot: Connects a laptop to a lock in order to prevent it from being stolen.

SD card slots and card readers: Used to accept digital memory cards found in digital cameras and similar technologies.

ExpressCard: Used to insert an ExpressCard to expand your computer's capabilities by offering additional ways to connect devices. ExpressCards are often used to offer wireless capabilities.

AV-in: Accepts input from various audio and video devices.

RF-in: Accepts input signal from digital TV tuners.

ALERT: On occasion, hardware manufacturers require you to install software first, so read the instructions that came with your hardware to know what order to do what, just as a precaution.

ALERT: If the hardware does not install properly, refer to the user manual.

2 First steps

Introduction

It's OK if you've never used a computer; that's what this chapter is about. Here you'll take your first steps, including turning on your PC. Once the computer has completed its startup process, you'll be able to use the computer by moving the mouse and typing on the keyboard.

If you have an older PC, you'll probably find that your computer has Windows XP installed on it. If you have a newer PC, it's more likely that it runs Windows Vista. These are both operating systems, the software that allows you to interact with the computer and installed hardware, using a graphical interface.

Start your PC

You start your PC by locating the power button and waiting for the startup process to complete. This startup process generally takes a minute or two, but on older PCs it can take longer. This process is called 'booting'.

1 Locate the power button on the tower or on the laptop.

2 Press the button.

3 If the monitor is not turned on or does not come on automatically, press the monitor's power button.

4 Wait for the computer to complete the boot process.

5 When the computer has finished booting, you will see the Desktop, which will look something like that shown here.

ALERT: During the boot process you may see a black screen, or a black screen with words on it, among other things.

ALERT: You may see a different picture or no picture at all, or you may be prompted to activate the computer and not yet have access to the Desktop.

Activate a new PC

If this is the first time you've started your new computer, you'll be prompted to enter some information. Specifically, you'll type your name, activate the operating system and, if desired, register your copy of Windows.

1. Follow the directions on the screen, clicking Next to move from one page of the activation wizard to the next.

2. When prompted to register, remember that registration is optional. You can skip this part if you want.

3. After you have activated the operating system, wait a few seconds for it to initialise.

4. Click the Start button at the bottom of the screen to view your user name.

ALERT: To activate and register Windows Vista during the initial set-up, you'll have to be connected to the Internet. Alternatively, you can use the phone number provide to activate over the phone.

ALERT: You may see something in addition to what's shown here, such as the Welcome Center in Windows Vista or a welcome page in Windows XP.

? DID YOU KNOW?
Activation is mandatory. If you do not activate Windows within the 30-day time frame, the computer will lose all functionality, except for the activation process.

? DID YOU KNOW?
Usually you can press Enter on the keyboard to activate Next on the screen.

SEE ALSO: Using the mouse is covered on pages 30–1.

Use the keyboard

The keyboard allows you to type letters, website addresses and the names of files you want to save. The keyboard also lets you move around the computer using the arrow keys, the Tab key and specialised keyboard features such as scroll wheels. There are also special keys; for example, F1 offers help when pressed.

1 Press the F1 key on the keyboard. Often this opens the Welcome Center (and sometimes Help and Support).

2 Press the Windows key. This often opens the Start menu. (Press this key again to hide the Start menu.)

3 Press the Tab key to move around the screen without using the mouse.

4 Press the Enter key to open any selected item.

HOT TIP: Single-click the mouse on the X in the top right corner of any window to close it.

Use the mouse

You use the mouse to move the pointer on the screen around the Desktop. Click the mouse once using the left mouse button to select any item. Double-click the left mouse button to open a file, folder or application. Click the mouse once using the right mouse button to access additional menus and information about what's under the mouse pointer.

1 Move the mouse around on the mouse pad. Notice that the mouse pointer moves on the screen.

2 Left-click the Start button at the bottom right to open the Start menu. (This is a single click.)

3 Left-click outside the Start menu in an empty area of the Desktop to hide the Start menu. (This is a single click.)

4 Position the mouse over the Recycle Bin.

5 Double-click the left mouse button quickly. This opens the Recycle Bin.

6 Single-click the X in the top right corner to close the Recycle Bin window.

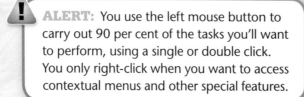

ALERT: You use the left mouse button to carry out 90 per cent of the tasks you'll want to perform, using a single or double click. You only right-click when you want to access contextual menus and other special features.

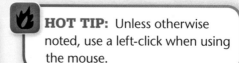

HOT TIP: Unless otherwise noted, use a left-click when using the mouse.

7 Position the mouse over the Recycle Bin again.

8 Right-click the mouse to see the contextual menu for the Recycle Bin. (This is a single click.)

9 Left-click an empty area of the Desktop to hide this menu. (This is a single click.)

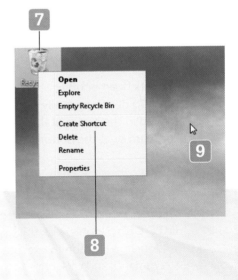

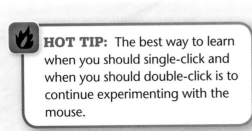

HOT TIP: The best way to learn when you should single-click and when you should double-click is to continue experimenting with the mouse.

Use the touchpad

When you open your laptop for the first time, you'll probably see a device for moving the mouse, usually a touchpad or trackball. You'll use this to move the mouse around the screen.

1 Place your finger on the touchpad or trackball and move your finger around. Notice that the mouse pointer moves.

2 If there are buttons, generally the left button functions in the same way as the left button on a mouse.

3 The right button functions in the same way as the right button of a mouse.

4 If there is a centre button, often this is used to scroll through pages. Try clicking and holding the button to move up, down, left or right on a page.

? DID YOU KNOW?

The touchpad or other pointing device is usually located in the centre of the keyboard or at the bottom of it.

HOT TIP: Right-click the left touchpad button to open contextual menus to access Properties, Copy, Select All and similar commands.

HOT TIP: Double-click the left touchpad button to execute a command, and click once to select something.

HOT TIP: Keep your fingers and hands clean when using the touchpad, as it has a sensitive surface.

View the Welcome Center in Vista

When you first start Windows Vista, the Welcome Center opens. (In Windows XP you'll see an option to take a tour.) There are at least two sections: *Get started with Windows* and *Offers from Microsoft*. There may also be others not included here.

1 With the Welcome Center open, view the items under Get Started with Windows.

2 Click What's new in Windows Vista.

3 If you do not want the Welcome Center to open every time you start Windows Vista, remove the tick mark from Run at startup.

Watch demonstration videos

Windows Vista offers demonstration videos. You may be interested in watching the videos regarding the basics. These video demonstrations show you how to use the mouse, use the Desktop, print, work with files, use the Web (Internet) and more.

1 Open the Welcome Center, and under Get started with Windows click Show all ___ items...

2 Double-click Windows Vista Demos.

3 Click Watch the demo to watch it.

4 To stop the demo, or to close Windows Media Player, click the X in Windows Media Player.

1. Get started with Windows (13)

View computer details   Transfer files and settings

Connect to the Internet   What's new in Windows Vista

Show all 13 items... **1**

HOT TIP: In Windows XP, choose Tour Windows XP (click Start, All Programs, Accessories, Tour Windows XP.)

? DID YOU KNOW?

The Welcome Center can be found by typing Welcome Center in the Start search window.

! ALERT: You may need to turn up your speakers to hear the demo.

WHAT DOES THIS MEAN?

Windows Media Center: A program that is included with Windows Vista for viewing videos, listening to music and viewing pictures.

Shut down Windows safely

When you're ready to turn off your computer, you need to do so using the method detailed here. Simply pressing the power button can damage the computer or the operating system.

1 Click Start.

2 Click the arrow shown here.

3 Click Shut Down.

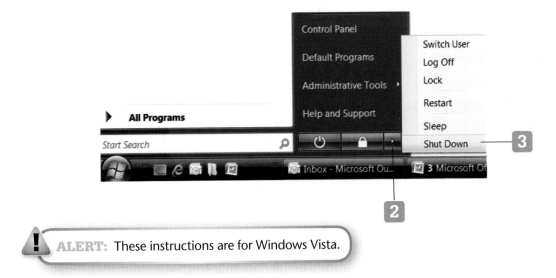

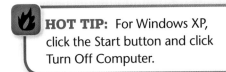
ALERT: These instructions are for Windows Vista.

HOT TIP: For Windows XP, click the Start button and click Turn Off Computer.

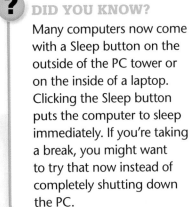
? DID YOU KNOW?
Many computers now come with a Sleep button on the outside of the PC tower or on the inside of a laptop. Clicking the Sleep button puts the computer to sleep immediately. If you're taking a break, you might want to try that now instead of completely shutting down the PC.

3 Common tasks

Introduction

You're probably ready to get started. To perform any task requires that you know where to begin. You'll begin at the Start menu. You'll use the Start menu to access tools such as the Calculator and applications such as Notepad. You can also locate games such as Solitaire, view sample pictures and listen to sample music available from your own personal folder. Once you're familiar with how to use the Start menu, you can then perform useful and fun tasks such as writing, saving and printing a letter, changing the picture on the Desktop and playing games.

Windows Vista is Microsoft's newest operating system (OS) and is the OS used throughout the rest of this book. If you have XP instead, don't worry: I'll include tips throughout the book to help you find your way.

Locate, open and close an application

An application is a program that allows you to perform a task, such as viewing a photo or playing a game. There are lots of applications included with both Windows Vista and Windows XP, including Notepad for writing letters, Calculator for performing mathematical calculations, Windows Media Player for listening to music and watching DVDs, and Paint for editing images and creating printouts and signs.

ALERT: To use an application, you must first locate it and then open it.

All Programs

Start Search

1 Click Start.

2 Click All Programs.

3 If necessary, use the scroll bars to browse the applications. Vista's All Programs menu is shown here.

4 Click Windows Media Player to open the application.

5 Click the X in the top right corner to close the application.

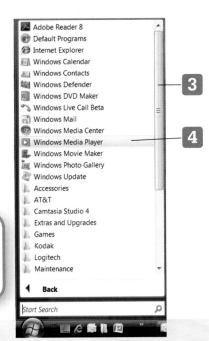

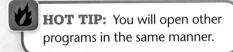

Media Guide

HOT TIP: In Windows XP, the All Programs menu looks different, but it still offers the same functionality.

HOT TIP: You will open other programs in the same manner.

DID YOU KNOW? To close most programs, you can also click File and then Exit.

Open a window

Each time you click something in the Start menu, in the All Programs menu or on the Desktop, a window opens to display its contents. The window will stay open until you close it.

1 Click Start.

2 Click your user name.

3 View the items in your personal folder.

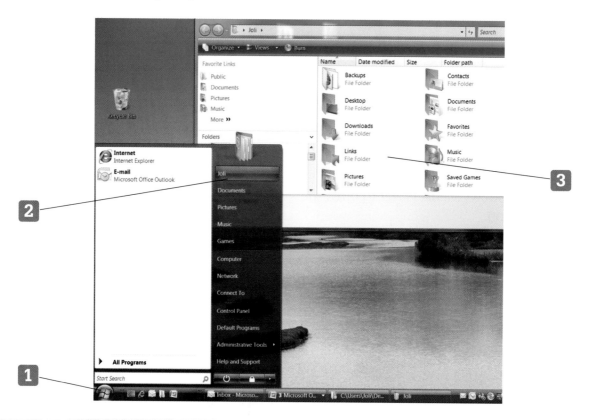

HOT TIP: Double-click any folder inside your personal folder to open it. Click the back arrow to return to the previous view (also called a window).

DID YOU KNOW?

If you see a red X in the top right corner, you're looking at a window. If you don't see a red X, the technical term for the item is often dialogue box.

Close a window

To close a window, click the X in the top right corner of it.

1 Click Start.

2 Click your user name. Your personal folder opens.

3 Click the X in the top right corner to close it.

Minimise button

3

HOT TIP: If you don't want to close the window but instead simply want to hide it, click the Minimise button – the dash to the left of the X in the top right corner.

Search for a program with the Start menu

To locate a program on your computer, you can search for the program using the Start Search window. Just type in what you want and then select the appropriate program from the list.

1 Click Start.

2 In the Start Search window, type Photo.

3 Note the results.

4 Click any result to open it. If you want to open Windows Photo Gallery, click it once. Note that it's under Programs.

? DID YOU KNOW?
This feature is only available in Windows Vista and is not available in Windows XP.

! ALERT: When you search using the Start Search window, all kinds of results may appear, not just programs.

HOT TIP: The easiest way to find something on your computer is to type it into the Start Search window.

? DID YOU KNOW?
You can search for programs in Windows XP by clicking Start and then Search.

Write a letter with Notepad

You can use Notepad to type a quick memo, note or letter. You can access Notepad from the Start menu.

1 Click Start.

2 In the Start Search window, type Notepad.

3 Click Notepad under Programs. (Note that you may see other results, as shown here.)

4 Click once inside Notepad, and start typing.

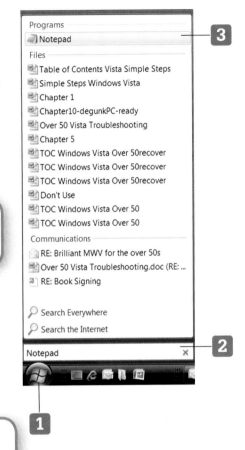

ALERT: Notepad has five menus: File, Edit, Format, View and Help. You can use these menus to save the letter, choose a font and more.

HOT TIP: To change the font or font size, select the typed text and click Format.

ALERT: If you close Notepad before saving or printing the file, your work will be lost.

Save a letter with Notepad

If you want to save a letter you've written in Notepad, you have to click File and then click Save. This will allow you to name the file and save it to your hard drive. The next time you want to view the file, you can click File and then click Open.

1 Click File.

2 Click Save.

3 Type a name for the file.

4 Click Save.

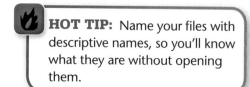

HOT TIP: Name your files with descriptive names, so you'll know what they are without opening them.

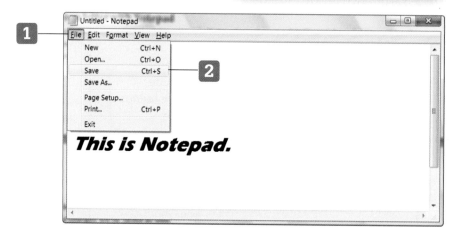

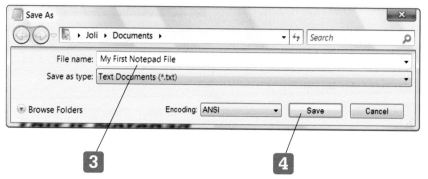

HOT TIP: By default, the file will be saved in your Documents folder. You can access this folder from the Start menu.

Reopen a saved file

You can reopen saved files easily. Just locate the file in the Documents folder, and double-click it.

1 Click Start.

2 Click Documents.

3 Double-click the file to open it.

? **DID YOU KNOW?**

In Windows XP, click Start and click My Documents. You'll find the file you want there.

? **DID YOU KNOW?**

You can save changes to the file if you make them by clicking the Save button on the toolbar.

Print a letter with Notepad

Sometimes you'll need to print a letter so you can post it. You can access the Print command from the File menu.

1 Click File.

2 Click Print.

3 Select a printer.

4 Click Print.

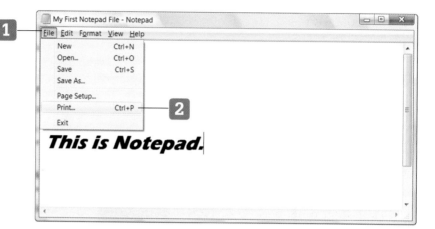

HOT TIP: You must have a printer installed, plugged in and turned on in order to print.

WHAT DOES THIS MEAN?

Printer Preferences: Lets you select the page orientation, print order and the type of paper you'll be printing on, among other features.

Page Range: Lets you select what specific pages to print.

Use the calculator

You've probably used a calculator before. Using Vista's or XP's calculator is not much different from a handheld one, except that you input numbers with a mouse click or key press. There are two calculator options: Standard and Scientific. The Standard calculator is the default and is a bare-bones version. The Scientific calculator offers many more features.

1 Click Start.

2 In the Start Search dialogue box, type Calculator.

3 In the Programs results, click Calculator.

4 Input numbers using the keypad, or input numbers by clicking the on-screen calculator with the mouse.

5 Input operations using the keypad, or input numbers by clicking the on-screen calculator with the mouse.

6 Close Calculator by clicking the X in the top right corner of it.

SEE ALSO: Opening an application is covered earlier in this chapter.

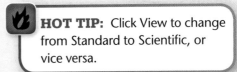 **HOT TIP:** Click View to change from Standard to Scientific, or vice versa.

Play solitaire

Windows Vista and Windows XP both come with lots of games. You access the available games from the Games folder on the Start menu. (In XP, click Start and then All Programs to access the Games folder.) Each game offers instructions on how to play it. Generally, moving a player, tile or card, dealing a card, and otherwise moving around the screen is performed using the mouse or arrow keys.

1 Click Start.

2 Click Games.

3 Double-click Solitaire to begin the game.

4 Double-click any card to move it, or drag the card to the desired location.

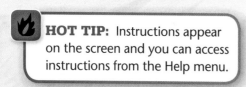

HOT TIP: Instructions appear on the screen and you can access instructions from the Help menu.

Change the background

One of the first things you may like to do when you get a new PC or upgrade an older one is to personalise the picture on the Desktop. That picture is called the background.

1 Right-click an empty area of the Desktop.

2 Click Personalise.

3 Click Desktop Background.

4 For Location, select Windows Wallpapers. If it not chosen already, click the down arrow to locate it.

5 Use the scroll bars to locate the wallpaper you want to use as your Desktop background.

6 Select a background to use.

7 Select a positioning option (the default is the most common).

8 Click OK.

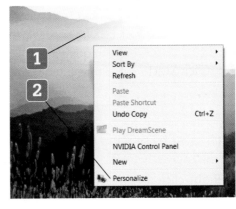

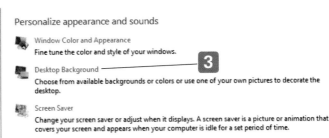

Personalize appearance and sounds

Window Color and Appearance
Fine tune the color and style of your windows.

Desktop Background — **3**
Choose from available backgrounds or colors or use one of your own pictures to decorate the desktop.

Screen Saver
Change your screen saver or adjust when it displays. A screen saver is a picture or animation that covers your screen and appears when your computer is idle for a set period of time.

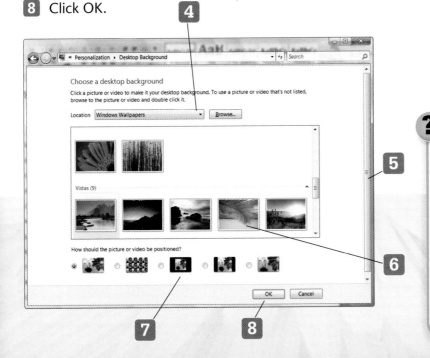

Change the screen saver

A screen saver is a picture or animation that covers your screen and appears after your
computer has been idle for a specific amount of time that you set. You disable the

ALERT: You can configure your screen saver to
require a password on waking up and thus keep
unwanted visitors from accessing your computer
while you're not using it.

screen saver by moving the mouse or pressing a key on the keyboard.

1 Right-click an empty area of
the desktop.

2 Click Personalise.

3 Click Screen Saver.

4 Click the arrow to see the available screen
savers, and then select one.

5 Use the arrows to change how long to wait
before the screen saver is enabled.

6 If desired, click On resume, display logon
screen to require a password to log back
into the computer.

7 Click OK.

 Screen Saver

Change your screen saver or adjust when it displays. A screen saver is a
picture or animation that covers your screen and appears when your
computer is idle for a set period of time.

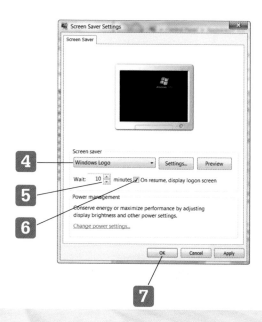

? DID YOU KNOW?

Select Photos and your screen
saver will be a slideshow of
photos stored in your Pictures
folder.

? DID YOU KNOW?

It used to be that screen
savers 'saved' your computer
screen from image burn-in,
but that is no longer the case.

Empty the Recycle Bin

The Recycle Bin holds deleted files until you decide to empty it. The Recycle Bin serves as a safeguard, allowing you to recover items that you have accidentally deleted and items that you thought you no longer wanted but later decide you need.

1. Locate the Recycle Bin on the Desktop and point to it with the mouse.

2. Right-click the Recycle Bin.

3. Choose Empty Recycle Bin.

4. Click Yes.

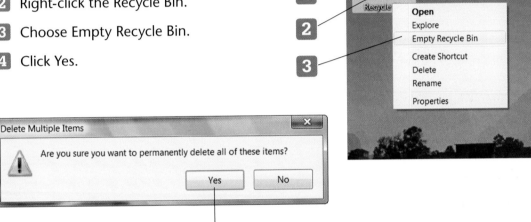

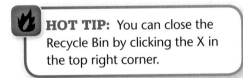

ALERT: Once you empty the Recycle Bin, the items in it are gone forever.

HOT TIP: You can close the Recycle Bin by clicking the X in the top right corner.

4 Work with files and folders

Introduction

When you use your computer, you often create and obtain data. These data can be letters, pictures, to-do lists, and even music and video that you get from the Internet. To keep the data on your computer so they're always available, you save the data. You save data as files, and you store files in folders. It's very similar to how you'd store data (documents and pictures) in a physical filing cabinet.

When you choose to save data, you're prompted by the operating system (XP or Vista) to save the data in a folder that represents the data you want to save. For instance, when saving a document, you're prompted to save it in the Documents folder; and when saving or uploading pictures, you're prompted to save them to the Pictures folder.

In this chapter you'll learn where files are saved by default, and how to create your own folders and subfolders for organising data. You'll also learn how to copy, move and delete files and folders, how to locate saved files, and how to perform searches for data when you can't find them.

Locate your personal folders

You should save data to your personal folders. In Vista, they're already created for you and include Pictures, Music, Documents, Video and Contacts, among others. In XP, those folders are named My Pictures, My Documents, My Videos, etc.

1 Click the Start menu.

2 Locate your user name.

3 Click it to open your personal folders (shown on page 58).

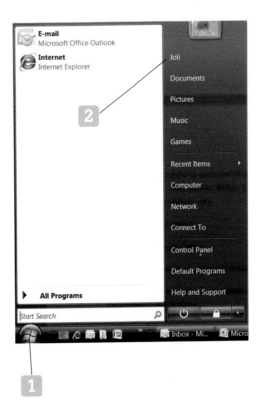

? **DID YOU KNOW?**

Vista offers more personal folders than XP, including Contacts (for storing information about other people) and Saved Games (for storing games you've added and purchased).

🔥 **HOT TIP:** When you're ready to save data, you're going to want to save the data to the folder that most closely matches the data you're saving. Documents belong in the Documents folder, and pictures belong in the Pictures folder.

? **DID YOU KNOW?**

You can access some of your personal folders directly from the Start menu, such as Documents and Pictures.

WHAT DOES THIS MEAN?

Your personal folder contains the following folders, which in turn contain data you've saved:

Contacts: This folder contains your contacts' information, which includes email addresses, pictures, phone numbers, home and businesses addresses, and more.

Desktop: This folder contains links to items for data you created on your desktop.

Documents: This folder contains saved documents, subfolders you've created and folders created by Vista, including Fax, My Received Files, Remote Assistance Logs and Scanned Documents.

Downloads: This folder does not contain anything by default. It does offer a place to save items you download from the Internet, such as drivers and third-party programs.

Favorites: This folder contains the items in Internet Explorer's Favorites list. It may also include folders created by the computer manufacturer or Microsoft, including Links, Microsoft Websites and MSN Websites.

Links: This folder contains shortcuts to the Documents, Music, Pictures, Public, Recently Changed and Searches folders.

Music: This folder contains sample music and music you save to the PC.

Pictures: This folder contains sample pictures and pictures you save to the PC.

Saved Games: This folder contains games that come with Windows Vista and offers a place to save extra games that you acquire.

Searches: This folder contains preconfigured search folders, including Recent Documents, Recent E-mail, Recent Music, Recent Pictures and Videos, Recently Changed, and Shared By Me. If you need to find something recently accessed or changed and don't know where to look, you can probably locate it here. These folders get updated each time you open them.

Videos: This folder contains sample videos and videos that you save to the PC.

Create a folder

Your personal folders, the ones already created in XP and Vista, will suit your needs for a while, but you may want to create folders of your own. You can create a folder on the Desktop to hold information you access often.

1 Right-click an empty area of your desktop.

2 Point to New.

3 Click Folder.

4 Type a name for the folder.

5 Press Enter on the keyboard.

HOT TIP: Create a folder to hold data related to a hobby, tax information, work or family.

ALERT: If you can't type a name for the folder, right-click the folder and select Rename.

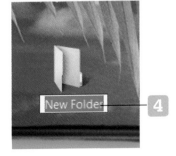

DID YOU KNOW?
You can drag the folder to another area of the Desktop or even to another area of the hard drive to move it there.

Create a subfolder

You can also create folders inside other folders. For instance, inside the Documents folder, you may want to create a subfolder called Tax Information to hold scanned receipts, tax records and account information. Inside the Pictures folder you might want to create folders named 2008, 2009, 2010, or Weddings, Holiday, Grandkids and so on.

1 Click Start.

2 Click your user name to open your personal folder.

3 Right-click an empty area inside the folder.

4 Point to New.

5 Click Folder.

6 Type a name for the folder.

7 Press Enter on the keyboard.

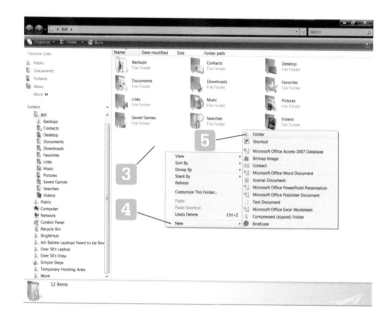

 ALERT: If you can't type a name for the folder, right-click the folder and select Rename.

 HOT TIP: Anything you create that is appropriate for this folder name should be saved here.

Copy a file

Folders contain files. Sometimes you'll need to copy a file to another location. Perhaps you want to copy the files to an external drive, memory card or USB thumb drive for the purpose of backing it up, or maybe you want to create a copy so you can edit the data in it without worrying about changing the original.

1 Locate a file to copy.

2 Right-click the file.

3 While holding down the right mouse key, drag the file to the new location.

4 Drop the file there.

5 Choose Copy Here.

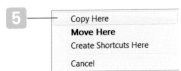

ALERT: To copy a file, you first have to browse to it. Open your personal folders to find a file to copy.

HOT TIP: If you don't have any files yet, you can locate a music file in the Music folder. Click Start, click Music and then open the Sample Music folder by double-clicking it.

DID YOU KNOW?
In the example, I'm copying a file to the Desktop. You can copy files to other folders using the same method, but you'll have to open the folder first.

DID YOU KNOW?
It might be helpful to think of folders and subfolders in a more physical way, as folders and subfolders in a filing cabinet. Folders on your computer help you keep your data organised and easily available, just as they do in a filing cabinet.

Move a file

When you copy something, an exact duplicate is made. For the most part, this is not what you want to do with data, unless you're backing things up. You generally want to move data. If a picture of a graduation needs to be put in the Graduation Pictures folder, you need to move it, not copy it.

1 Locate a file that you want to move.

2 Right-click the file.

3 While holding down the right mouse key, drag the file to the new location.

4 Drop the file there.

5 Choose Move Here.

Forest Flowers   Frangipani Flowers   Garden

HOT TIP: You move a file in the same way that you copy one, except when you drop the file you choose Move Here instead of Copy Here.

? **DID YOU KNOW?**
In the example, I'm moving a file to the Desktop. You can move files to other folders using the same method, but you'll have to open the folder first.

HOT TIP: To put the file back in its original location, repeat these steps, dragging the file from the Desktop back to the Sample Pictures folder.

Delete a file

When you are sure you no longer need a particular file, you can delete it. Deleting a file sends it to the Recycle Bin. This file can be restored if you decide you need it later, provided that you have not emptied the Recycle Bin since deleting the file.

1 Locate a file to delete.

2 Right-click the file.

3 Choose Delete.

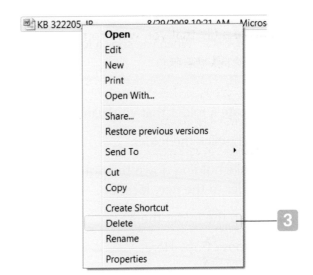

DID YOU KNOW?

It's best to keep unwanted or unnecessary data off your hard drive. That means you should delete data you don't need, including items in the Recycle Bin.

Copy a folder

Folders often contain other folders (subfolders). Sometimes you'll need to copy a folder to another location. Perhaps you want to copy the folder to an external drive, memory card or USB thumb drive for the purpose of backing it up, or maybe you want to create a copy so you can edit the data in it without worrying about changing the original.

ALERT: When you copy a folder, you copy all of the data inside it.

Sample Pictures

: 5/15/2008 9:26 AM
: Everyone

1 Locate a folder that you want to copy.

2 Right-click the folder.

3 While holding down the right mouse key, drag the folder to the new location.

4 Drop the folder there.

5 Choose Copy Here.

ALERT: To delete the copy, right-click it and choose Delete.

5

| Copy Here |
| **Move Here** |
| Create Shortcuts Here |
| Cancel |

? DID YOU KNOW?

When you delete a copy of a folder, the original folder remains intact.

Move a folder

If you have created a folder on your Desktop, you may want to move the folder and its contents to your personal folder.

1. Locate a folder to move.

2. Open the folder that you want to move it to. (For instance, open your personal folder by clicking your name on the Start menu.)

3. Right-click the folder.

4. While holding down the right mouse key, drag the file to the new location.

5. Drop the folder there.

6. Choose Move Here.

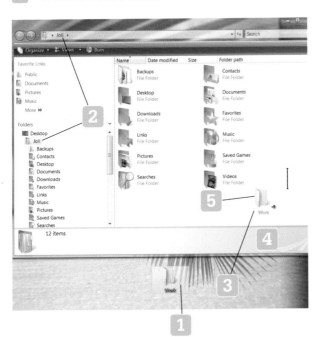

? DID YOU KNOW?
Keeping all of your data in your personal folders will help keep to your Desktop uncluttered. It also makes backing up the data later easier, because all of your data are in one place.

? DID YOU KNOW?
You may have to open a folder in order to locate the folder you want to move.

🔥 HOT TIP: I suggest that you move the folder you created on your Desktop earlier to your personal folder (if you're working through this chapter sequentially, anyway).

🔥 HOT TIP: To put the folder back in its original location, repeat these steps, dragging the folder from the Desktop back to its original location.

Delete a folder

When you are sure that you no longer need a particular folder, you can delete it. When you delete a folder, you delete the folder and everything in it. Deleting a folder sends it and its contents to the Recycle Bin. The folder can be restored if you decide you need it later, provided that you have not emptied the Recycle Bin since deleting the folder.

1 Locate a folder to delete.

2 Right-click the folder.

3 Choose Delete.

? DID YOU KNOW?

It's best to keep unwanted or unnecessary data off your hard drive. That means you should delete data you don't need, including items in the Recycle Bin.

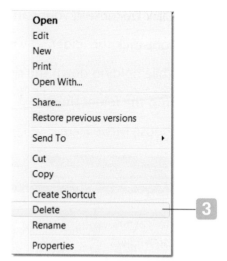

Open
Edit
New
Print
Open With...

Share...
Restore previous versions

Send To   ▸

Cut
Copy

Create Shortcut
Delete ————— 3
Rename

Properties

Open a saved file

Once data (in this case, a file) are saved to your hard drive, you can access, and often modify, the data. Most of the time, you open a saved file from a personal folder or a folder you've created.

1. Click Start.

2. Click Documents.

3. Locate the file that you want to open in the Documents folder.

4. Double-click it to open it.

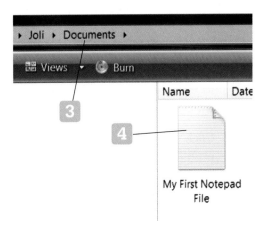

My First Notepad File

SEE ALSO: Review the sections Write a letter with Notepad and Save a letter with Notepad in Chapter 3 to learn how to create and save a text file.

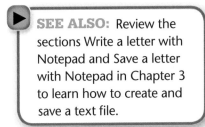

? DID YOU KNOW?
The file will open in the appropriate program automatically.

Search for a lost file

After you create data, such as a Notepad document, you save the data to your hard drive. When you're ready to use the file again, you have to locate it and open it. If you know that the document is in the Documents folder, you can click Start and then click Documents. Then you can simply double-click the file to open it. However, if you aren't sure where the file is, you'll have to search for it.

1 Click Start.

2 In Vista, in the Start Search window, type the name of the file.

3 Click the file to open it. There will be multiple search results.

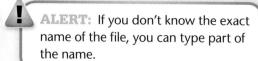

? DID YOU KNOW?

Windows XP does not have a Start Search window, and you'll have to use a different method: click Start, click Search, and then use the available search tools there.

? DID YOU KNOW?

If you don't know any part of the name of the file, you can type a word that is included inside the file or a specific type of file.

! ALERT: If you don't know the exact name of the file, you can type part of the name.

Back up a folder or file to an external drive

Once you have your data saved in folders, you can copy the folders to an external drive to create a back-up. You copy the folder to the external drive in the same way as you copy a folder to another area of your hard drive: you open both folders and drag and drop.

1 Click Start and click Computer.

2 Locate the external drive. (Leave this window open and resize it so that it takes up only part of the screen.)

3 Locate a folder (or folders) to copy. Resize this window as shown here, so that you can drag and drop between the two open windows.

4 Position the windows so you can see them both.

5 Right-click the folder to copy.

6 While holding down the right mouse key, drag the folder to the new location.

7 Drop the folder there.

8 Choose Copy Here.

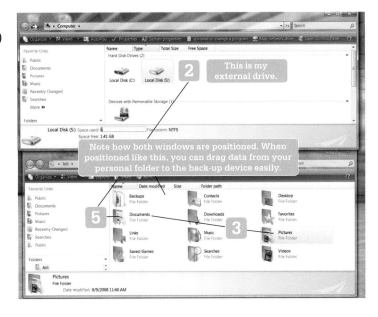

SEE ALSO: Resizing and restoring a window is covered in Chapter 6.

HOT TIP: Click Start and click your personal folder (the one with your name on it) to locate a folder to copy.

HOT TIP: You can also drag a single file to a back-up device, if desired.

ALERT: Before you begin, plug in or attach the external drive.

5 Personalise Vista

Introduction

Now that you've spent some time on tasks that you should know how to do, let's take a break and do some things you want to know how to do. This is the fun stuff, such as using Vista's Sidebar, using Vista's Aero and changing how Vista looks.

If you have XP, pay attention to the alerts boxes in the chapter. XP doesn't offer Aero, the Sidebar or Flip 3D, although you can change the screen resolution, use Flip and change the picture on the Start menu.

Enable the Sidebar

Windows Sidebar is a nifty feature that sits on your desktop and offers information on the weather, time and date, and gives you access to your contacts and other data. You can even have a slideshow of your favourite pictures. By default, the Sidebar is enabled. If you can see the Sidebar, skip this section.

1 If the Sidebar is not on the Desktop, click Start.

2 In the Start Search window, type Sidebar.

3 Under Programs, click Windows Sidebar. The sidebar is shown on the next page.

! **ALERT:** XP does not offer the Sidebar.

! **ALERT:** You won't get up-to-date information on the weather, clock and other real-time gadgets unless you're connected to the Internet.

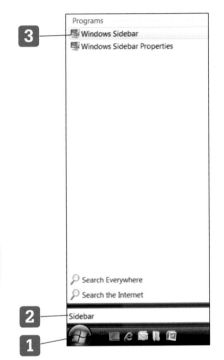

Set the time on the clock gadget

Almost all gadgets on the Sidebar offer up a wrench icon when you position your mouse over them. You can use this icon to access settings for the gadget. The first thing you may want to set is the time on the clock gadget.

1 Position the mouse pointer over the clock in the Sidebar. Look for the small x and the wrench to appear.

2 Click the arrow in the Time zone window and select your time zone from the list.

3 Click the right arrow underneath the clock to change the clock type.

4 Click OK.

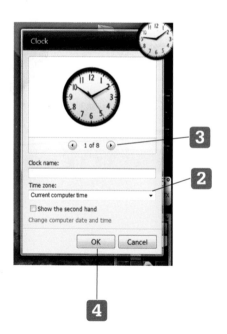

HOT TIP: Clicking the x will remove the gadget from the Sidebar. Clicking the wrench will open the gadget's properties, if properties are available.

SEE ALSO: The Sidebar must be enabled in order to access the clock icon. To enable the Sidebar, refer to the previous section.

ALERT: The Stocks gadget runs about 15 minutes behind real-time stock data, so don't start buying and selling based on what you see here.

Add or remove a Sidebar gadget

Windows Vista comes with several gadgets in its Gadget Gallery, allowing you to add gadgets easily. You can remove gadgets from the Sidebar by clicking the x icon that appears when you hover the mouse over them.

1 To add a gadget, right-click an empty area of the Sidebar.

2 Click Add Gadgets.

3 In the Gadget Gallery, drag the gadget you want to add to the Sidebar and drop it there. (Repeat as desired.)

4 Click the X in the Gadget Gallery to close it.

5 Click the X in any gadget to remove it from the Sidebar. This does not remove the gadget from the computer. Remember that the X will not appear until you hover the mouse over it.

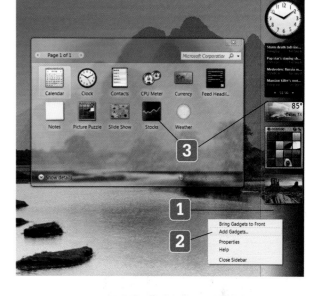

ALERT: XP does not offer the Sidebar or the Gadget Gallery.

ALERT: Although you can get gadgets online, make sure you read the reviews of the gadgets you want before downloading and installing them, as they could be buggy or dangerous. Don't be afraid to get gadgets online: just be careful and read the reviews before installing.

? DID YOU KNOW?

Right-click an empty area of the Sidebar and select Properties to change what side of the Desktop the Sidebar appears on.

Close the Sidebar

Not everyone likes the Sidebar. If you want to close it, use a right-click.

1 Right-click an empty area of the Sidebar.

2 Click Close Sidebar.

> **? DID YOU KNOW?**
>
> You can show the Sidebar by clicking the Sidebar icon on the taskbar. The taskbar is the grey bar that runs across the bottom of your screen.

Bring Gadgets to Front
Add Gadgets...

Properties
Help

Close Sidebar

2

Enable Aero

Aero is an interface enhancement that you can enable for a cleaner, sleeker interface and Vista experience. Windows Aero offers a high-performing desktop experience that includes, among other things, the translucent effect of Aero Glass and Flip 3D.

1 Right-click an empty area of the Desktop.

2 Click Personalise.

3 Click Window Color and Appearance.

4 If you're not using Aero already, you'll see the Appearance Settings dialogue box. If you're currently using Windows Aero, you'll see the Aero options shown here.

5 To change from Windows Vista Basic to Windows Aero, click Windows Aero in the Color Scheme options, and then click OK.

ALERT: Your computer must meet some minimum requirements in order for you to use Aero. You must be running Windows Vista Home Premium, Ultimate or Business, and your graphics card must meet Aero's resource needs.

? DID YOU KNOW?
You don't have to use Aero. If you prefer the basic Vista experience, you can turn this feature off.

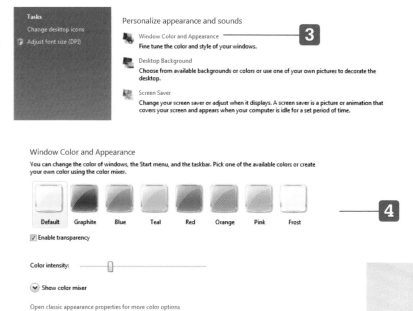

Tasks
Change desktop icons
Adjust font size (DPI)

Personalize appearance and sounds

Window Color and Appearance — **3**
Fine tune the color and style of your windows.

Desktop Background
Choose from available backgrounds or colors or use one of your own pictures to decorate the desktop.

Screen Saver
Change your screen saver or adjust when it displays. A screen saver is a picture or animation that covers your screen and appears when your computer is idle for a set period of time.

Window Color and Appearance

You can change the color of windows, the Start menu, and the taskbar. Pick one of the available colors or create your own color using the color mixer.

Default   Graphite   Blue   Teal   Red   Orange   Pink   Frost   — **4**

☑ Enable transparency

Color intensity:

⊙ Show color mixer

Open classic appearance properties for more color options

OK   Cancel

Use Flip

Windows Flip 3D offers a quick way to choose a specific window when multiple windows are open, by offering the ability to move among program icons using a one-dimensional interface. With Flip, you can scroll through open windows until you land on the one you want to use, and then select it.

1 With multiple windows open, on the keyboard hold down the Alt key with one finger or thumb.

2 Press and hold the Tab key.

3 Press the Tab key again, making sure that the Alt key is still depressed.

4 When the item you want to bring to the front is selected, let go of the Tab key and then let go of the Alt key.

C:\Users\Joli\Pictures

 HOT TIP: The Alt key is to the left of the space bar. The Tab key is to the left of the Q.

 ALERT: XP has its own version of Flip that looks similar to this.

Use Flip 3D

Windows Flip 3D offers a quick way to choose a specific window when multiple windows are open by offering the ability to move among program icons using a three-dimensional interface. With Flip, you can scroll through open windows until you land on the one you want to use, and then select it. Only Vista offers Flip 3D.

1 With multiple windows open, on the keyboard hold down the Windows key (which may have Start written on it) with one finger or thumb.

2 Click the Tab key once, while keeping the Alt key depressed.

3 Press the Tab key again, making sure that the Alt key is still depressed, to scroll through the open windows.

4 When the item you want to bring to the front is selected, let go of the Tab key and then let go of the Alt key.

 HOT TIP: The Windows key is the key to the left of the space bar. It has the Windows logo printed on it.

 ALERT: If Flip 3D doesn't work, or if you get only Flip and not Flip 3D, either your PC does not support Aero or it is not configured to use it.

Change the screen resolution

Screen resolution defines how many pixels appear on your screen. When you increase the resolution, you increase the number of pixels on the screen. This makes items on the screen appear smaller and allows you to have more items on screen.

1 Right-click an empty area of the Desktop.

2 Click Personalize.

3 Click Display Settings.

4 Move the Resolution slider to the far left position, unless it's already there.

5 Click Apply.

6 When prompted to keep this setting, choose Yes or No.

 DID YOU KNOW?

Technically, choosing 800 × 600 pixels means that the Desktop is shown with 800 pixels across and 600 pixels down. Choosing 1280 × 1024 means there are 1280 pixels across and 1024 down.

 Display Settings

Adjust your monitor resolution, which changes the view so more or fewer items fit on the screen. You can also control monitor flicker (refresh rate).

WHAT DOES THIS MEAN?

Pixel: The smallest unit of data that can be displayed on a computer.

Change the picture on the Start menu

The picture on your Start menu is the picture applied to your user name. To change your picture, simply click the picture and choose a new one.

1 Click Start.

2 Click the picture on the top of the Start menu.

3 Click Change your picture.

4 Select a new picture.

5 Click Change Picture.

Choose a new picture for your account

Joli
Administrator
Password protected

The picture you choose will appear on the Welcome screen and on the Start menu.

Browse for more pictures...

4

5 — Change Picture | Cancel

ALERT: These are the steps for Vista, but XP uses a similar procedure.

? DID YOU KNOW?
When you change your picture here, you change the picture for your user name too.

HOT TIP: Close the Control Panel by clicking the X in the top right corner.

Get recommendations to make your computer easier to use

If you find it difficult to use your PC effectively because of a disability such as a hearing, vision or dexterity problem, Vista can help.

1 Click Start, and in the Start Search window type Ease.

2 Under Programs, click Ease of Access Center.

3 Click Get recommendations to make your computer easier to use.

4 Answer the questions as they are asked, clicking Next to move to the next screen.

5 Configure the recommended settings in the Ease of Access Center.

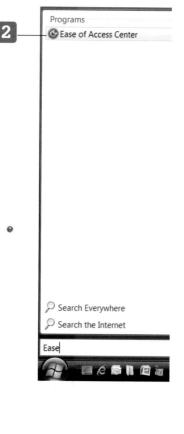

 ALERT: This section applies only to Vista users.

6 Work with windows

Introduction

So far you've learned quite a bit about your computer and how to use it. What you haven't learned is how to work with windows. The term 'window', as it is used in this chapter, is not capitalised and does not have anything to do with any product name (for instance, Microsoft Windows XP or Microsoft Windows Vista). Here, the term 'windows' is used to represent a part of the interface that you will use to access files inside a folder window, menus inside an application window and settings available in the Control Panel window.

To work with windows requires you to know how to resize, move and arrange open windows on your desktop. This is essential because each time you open a program, file, folder, picture or anything else, almost always a new window opens. You have to be very familiar with these windows, including how to show and hide them, in order to become comfortable navigating your computer.

Change the view in a window

When you open your personal folder from the Start menu, you will see additional folders inside it. You can open any of these subfolders to see what's in them. You can change what the content inside these folders looks like. You can configure each folder independently so that the data appear in a list, as small icons and as large icons, to name just a few options.

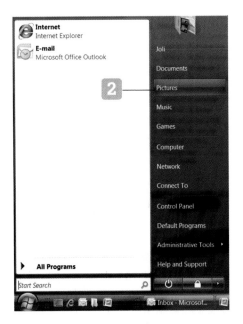

1 Click Start.

2 Click Pictures.

3 Click the arrow next to Views.

4 Move the slider to select an option from the list.

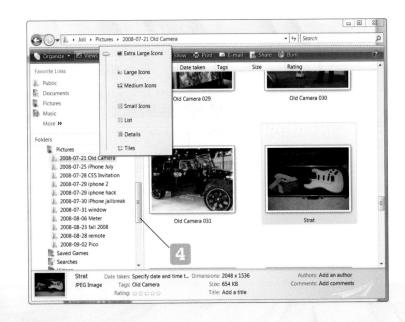

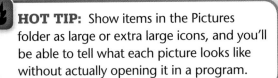

HOT TIP: Show items in the Pictures folder as large or extra large icons, and you'll be able to tell what each picture looks like without actually opening it in a program.

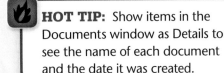

HOT TIP: Show items in the Documents window as Details to see the name of each document and the date it was created.

Minimise a window

When you have several open windows, you may want to minimise (hide) the windows that you aren't using. A minimised window appears on the taskbar as a small icon and is not on the Desktop. When you're ready to use the window again, you simply click it.

1 Open any window. (Click Start, and then click Pictures, Documents, Games or any other option.)

2 Click the – sign in the top right corner.

3 Locate the window title in the taskbar. Position your mouse over the icon to see its thumbnail.

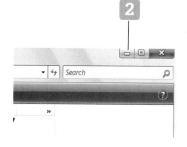

> **!** **ALERT:** A minimised window is on the taskbar and is not shown on the Desktop. You can restore the window by clicking on its icon on the taskbar. Restoring a window to the Desktop brings the window back up so you can work with it.

> **!** **ALERT:** You won't see the thumbnail shown here unless you have Aero enabled. (See Enable Aero in Chapter 5.)

WHAT DOES THIS MEAN?

Taskbar: The grey bar that runs across the bottom of your screen. It contains the Start button and the Notification area.

Restore a window

A window can be minimised (on the taskbar), maximised (filling the entire Desktop) or in restore mode (not maximised or minimised, but showing on the Desktop). When a window is in restore mode, you can resize or move the window as desired. You cannot resize or move windows that are minimised or maximised.

1 Open any window.

2 In the top right corner of the window, locate the two square buttons.

3 Click the button to put the window in restore mode.

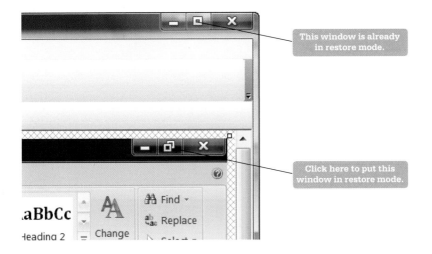

This window is already in restore mode.

Click here to put this window in restore mode.

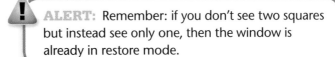

ALERT: Remember: if you don't see two squares but instead see only one, then the window is already in restore mode.

ALERT: In order to put a window in restore mode, you have to have access to the restore button. The restore button is made up of two squares that appear next to the X in the top right corner of any window. Clicking this button will put the window in restore mode. Once in restore mode, you can resize or move the window. If the icon next to the X in the top right corner of a window is a single square, then the window is already in restore mode and the only thing you can do is minimise or maximise it.

Maximise a window

A maximised window is as large as it can be and takes up the entire screen. You can maximise a window that is on the Desktop by clicking the square icon in the top right corner. If the icon is already a square, then it's already maximised.

1 Open any window.

2 In the top right corner of the window, locate the square.

3 Click it to maximise the window.

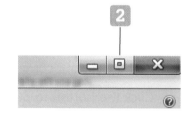

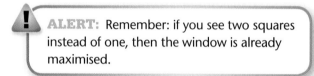

ALERT: Remember: if you see two squares instead of one, then the window is already maximised.

Move a window

You can move a window as long as it's in restore mode. You move a window by dragging it from its title bar. The title bar is the bar that runs across the top of the window. Moving windows allows you to position multiple windows across the screen.

1. Open any window.

2. Put the window in restore mode (if it is not already).

3. Left-click with the mouse on the title bar and drag. Let go of the mouse when the window is positioned correctly.

DID YOU KNOW?

You can open a document or a picture and it will open in a window.

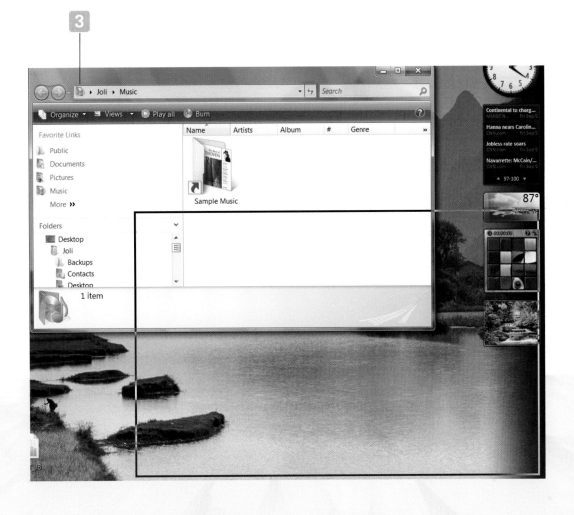

Resize a window

Resizing a window allows you to change the dimensions of the window. You can resize a window by dragging from its sides, corners, or the top and bottom.

1 Open any window. (If you're unsure, click Start and then Pictures.)

2 Put the window in restore mode. You want the maximise button to show.

3 Position the mouse at one of the window corners, so that the mouse pointer becomes a two-pointed arrow.

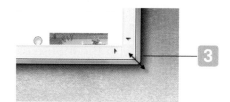
3

4 Hold down the mouse button and drag the arrow to resize the window.

5 Repeat as desired, dragging from the sides, top, bottom or corners.

ALERT: You can move and resize windows only if they are in restore mode, meaning that the maximise button is showing in the top right corner of the window.

7 The Internet

Introduction

The Internet is a vast network of computers. These computers offer websites and webpages that contain information, pictures, videos, hyperlinks to other websites, and more. These networks and computers are maintained by various entities, including large and small companies and individuals. Websites are stored on Web servers, which are available to people all over the world.

To access the Internet, you must connect to it. You can either use a free hotspot and a laptop (you'll find free hotspots in local coffee shops, libraries and hotels), or you will have to subscribe to a service called an ISP (Internet Service Provider) for a monthly fee and then log on to the Internet using a user name and password.

Before reading this chapter, make sure you are connected to the Internet. Note that this may require you to pay for and set up the service in your home or trek out to your local hotspot with a laptop.

Open a website in Internet Explorer

Windows Vista comes with Internet Explorer, an application you can use to surf the Internet. Internet Explorer is a web browser, and it has everything you need, including an application to block annoying pop-ups and the ability to save your favourite webpages. You'll use Internet Explorer to surf the Internet.

1 Open Internet Explorer. A website will probably open automatically.

2 To open a new website, drag your mouse across the website name to select it. Do not drag your mouse over the http://www part of the address.

3 Type the name of the website you'd like to visit in the address bar. Try http://www.amazon.com.

4 Press Enter on the keyboard.

WHAT DOES THIS MEAN?

Web browser: An application that allows you to view webpages.

Pop-up: An advertisement that appears and opens in its own window when you open some webpages on the Internet.

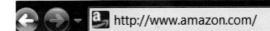

WHAT DOES THIS MEAN?

Address bar: Used to type in Internet addresses, also known as URLs (uniform resource locators). Generally, an Internet address takes the form of http://www.*companyname*.com.

 HOT TIP: You can open Internet Explorer from the Start menu or Quick Launch toolbar. Just look for the blue E.

 ALERT: Websites almost always start with http://www.

? **DID YOU KNOW?**

.com is the most popular website ending; it means that the website is a company, business or personal website. .edu is used for educational institutions, .gov mostly for government entities, .org mostly for non-profit organisations and .net for miscellaneous business and companies and personal websites. There are others as well, including .info, .biz, .tv and .uk.com.

Open a website in a new tab

You can open more than one website at a time in Internet Explorer. To do this, click the tab that appears to the right of the open webpage. Then type the name of the website you'd like to visit.

1 Open Internet Explorer.

2 Click an empty tab.

3 Type the name of the website you'd like to visit in the address bar.

4 Press Enter on the keyboard.

WHAT DOES THIS MEAN?

The Internet Explorer interface has several distinct parts:

Command bar: Used to access icons such as the Home and Print icons.

Tabs: Used to access websites when multiple sites are open.

Search window: Used to search for anything on the Internet.

 **HOT TIP:** Type the following: http://www.microsoft.com/uk.

 **DID YOU KNOW?**

When a website name starts with https://, it means that it's secure. When purchasing items online, make sure the payment pages have this prefix.

Set a home page

You can select a single webpage or multiple webpages to be displayed each time you open Internet Explorer. In fact, there are three options for configuring home pages:

- **Use this webpage as your only home page**: select this option if you want only one page to serve as your home page.

- **Add this webpage to your home pages tabs**: select this option if you want this page to be one of several home pages.

- **Use the current tab set as your home page**: select this option if you've opened multiple tabs and you want all of them to be home pages.

1 Use the Address bar to locate a webpage that you want to use as your home page.

2 Click the arrow next to the Home icon.

3 Click Add or Change Home Page.

4 Make a selection using the information provided regarding each option.

5 Click Yes.

6 Repeat these steps as desired.

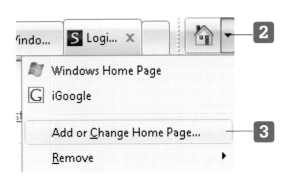

SEE ALSO: Opening a website in Internet Explorer is covered earlier in this chapter.

ALERT: You have to locate the webpage before you can assign it as a home page.

Mark a favourite

Favourites are websites that you save links to so you can access them more easily at a later time. Favourites differ from home pages because, by default, they do not open when you start Internet Explorer. The favourites you save appear in the Favorites Center, which you can access by clicking the large yellow star on the Command bar.

1 Go to the webpage you want to configure as a favourite.

2 Click the Add to Favourites icon.

3 To add a single webpage as a favourite, click Add to Favourites.

4 Type a name for the website when prompted.

5 Click Add.

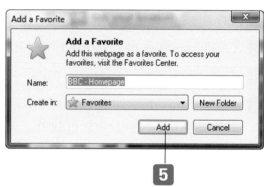

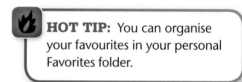

? DID YOU KNOW?

You will see some favourites listed, including Microsoft Websites and MSN Websites. Every time you save a favourite, it will appear here.

HOT TIP: You can organise your favourites in your personal Favorites folder.

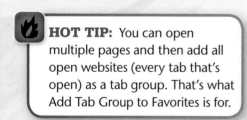

HOT TIP: You can open multiple pages and then add all open websites (every tab that's open) as a tab group. That's what Add Tab Group to Favorites is for.

Change the zoom level of a webpage

If you have trouble reading what's on a webpage because the text is too small, use the Page Zoom feature. Page Zoom works by preserving the fundamental design of the webpage you're viewing. This means that Page Zoom intelligently zooms in on the entire page, which maintains the page's integrity, layout and look.

1 Open Internet Explorer and browse to a webpage.

2 Click the arrow located at the bottom right of Internet Explorer to show the Zoom options.

3 Click 150%.

4 Notice how the webpage text and images increase in size. Use the scroll bars to navigate the page.

Clear history

If you don't want people to be able to snoop around on your computer and find out what sites you've been visiting, you'll need to delete your browsing history. Deleting your browsing history lets you remove the information stored on your computer related to your Internet activities.

1 Open Internet Explorer.

2 Click the Alt key on the keyboard.

3 Click Tools.

4 Click Delete Browsing History.

5 To delete any or all of the listed items, click the Delete button.

6 Click Close when finished.

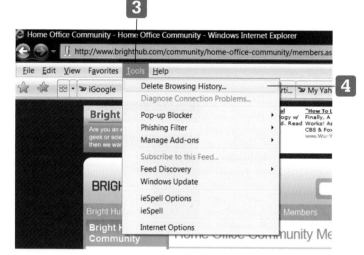

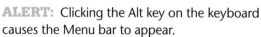

ALERT: Clicking the Alt key on the keyboard causes the Menu bar to appear.

WHAT DOES THIS MEAN?

Temporary Internet Files: These are files that have been downloaded and saved in your Temporary Internet Files folder. A snooper could go through these files to see what you've been doing online.

Cookies: These are small text files that include data to identify your preferences when you visit particular websites. Cookies allow you to visit, say, www.amazon.com and be greeted with Hello <your name>, We have recommendations for you! Cookies help a site offer you a personalised Web experience.

History: This is the list of websites you've visited and any Web addresses you've typed. Anyone can look at your History list to see where you've been.

Form data: This is information that's been saved using Internet Explorer's autocomplete form data functionality. If you don't want forms to be filled out automatically by you or someone else who has access to your PC and user account, delete this option.

Passwords: Passwords that were saved using Internet Explorer autocomplete password prompts.

Stay safe online

Staying secure when online and surfing the Internet has more to do with common sense than built-in security features. When you're online, make sure you follow the guidelines given here.

- If you are connecting to a public network, make sure you select Public when prompted by Windows Vista.

- Always keep your PC secure with antivirus software.

- Limit the amount of confidential information you store on the Internet.

- When making credit-card purchases and travel reservations, always make sure the website address starts with https://.

- Always sign out of any secure website you enter.

- Keep drinks, pets and cigarette smoke away from your PC.

 DID YOU KNOW?
When you connect to a network you know, such as a network in your home, you select Home or Work.

 ALERT: You have to purchase and install your own antivirus software, as it does not come with Vista.

Joli Ballew | **Edit Profile** | Writer Dashboard | Sign out

ALERT: Don't put your address and phone number on Facebook and other social networking sites.

 HOT TIP: The s after http lets you know it's a secure site.

WHAT DOES THIS MEAN?

Favourite: A webpage that you've chosen to maintain a shortcut for in the Favorites Center.

Home page: The webpage that opens when you open Internet Explorer. You can set the home page and configure additional pages to open as well.

Link: A shortcut to a webpage. Links are often offered in emails, documents and webpages to allow you to access a site without having to actually type in its name. In almost all instances, links are underlined and in a different colour from the page they are configured on.

Load: A webpage must 'load' before you can access it. Some pages load instantly, while others take a few seconds.

Navigate: The process of moving from one webpage to another or viewing items on a single webpage. Often the term is used as follows: 'click the link to navigate to the new webpage'.

Search: A term used when you type a word or group of words into a search window. Searching for data produces results.

Scroll up and scroll down: A process of using the scroll bars on a webpage or the arrow keys on a keyboard to move up and down the pages of a website.

Website: A group of webpages that contain related information. Microsoft's website contains information about Microsoft products, for instance.

URL: The information you type to access a website, such as http://www.microsoft.com.

Print a webpage

To print a webpage, simply click the Print icon on the Command bar.

1 Open Internet Explorer and browse to a webpage.

2 Click the Print icon on the command bar.

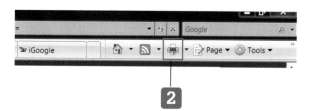

2

WHAT DOES THIS MEAN?

There are three menu options under the Print icon:

Print: Clicking Print opens the Print dialogue box, where you can configure the page range, select a printer, change page orientation, change print order and choose a paper type. Additional options include print quality and output bins. Of course, the choices offered depend on what your printer offers. If your printer can only print at 300 × 300 dots per inch (dpi), then you can't configure it to print at a higher quality.

Print Preview: Clicking this opens a window where you can see before you print what the printout will actually look like. You can switch between portrait and landscape views, access the Page Setup dialogue box and more.

Page Setup: Clicking this opens the Page Setup dialogue box. Here, you can select a paper size and source, and create headers and footers. You can also change orientation and margins, depending on what features your printer supports.

 HOT TIP: To access additional print options, click the arrow next to the Print icon.

8 Email

Introduction

Both Windows XP and Windows Vista come with an email program. In XP, the program is Outlook Express; in Vista, it's Windows Mail. With both of these email programs you can set up an email account using information obtained from your Internet service provider (ISP), and then view, reply to and compose emails. You can attach files too, including pictures and documents. You can also use built-in junk email filters, create folders for organising and storing email and manage your contacts.

In this chapter I'll introduce Windows Mail, but Outlook Express is quite similar.

Set up an email account in Windows Mail

The first time you open Windows Mail you'll be prompted to input the required information regarding your email address and email server. Windows Mail is a program for sending and receiving email, and you can't do that without inputting the proper information.

1 Click Start, and click Windows Mail.

2 Click Email Account. Click Next.

3 Type your display name. Click Next.

4 Type your email address. Click Next.

5 Fill in the information for your incoming and outgoing mail servers. Click Next.

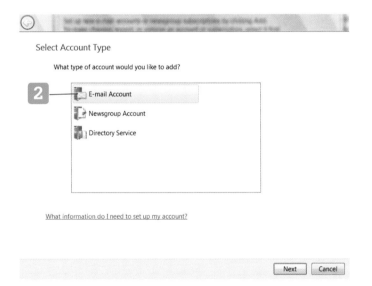

Select Account Type

What type of account would you like to add?

2 — E-mail Account

Newsgroup Account

Directory Service

What information do I need to set up my account?

Next   Cancel

WHAT DOES THIS MEAN?

Display name: This is the name that will appear in the From field when you compose an email, and in the recipient's inbox (under From in their email list) when they receive email from you. Don't put your email address here; put your first and last name, and any additional information.

6 Type your email username and password. Click Next.

7 Click Finish.

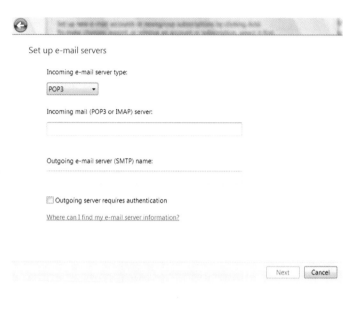

Set up e-mail servers

Incoming e-mail server type:

POP3

Incoming mail (POP3 or IMAP) server:

Outgoing e-mail server (SMTP) name:

☐ Outgoing server requires authentication

Where can I find my e-mail server information?

Next   Cancel

ALERT: If your ISP
told you that your
outgoing server requires
authentication, then tick
this box. If you aren't sure,
don't tick it.

ALERT: If you don't
know what to type, call
your ISP or visit their
website.

🔥 **HOT TIP:** Leave Remember
Password ticked and Mail will
remember it.

WHAT DOES THIS MEAN?

Email address: The email address you chose when you signed up with your ISP. It
often takes this form: *yourname@yourispname.com*.

Email user name and password: Often your user name is your email address.
Passwords are a security measure and are case-sensitive.

View an email

Windows Mail checks for email automatically when you first open the program and every 30 minutes thereafter. If you want to check for email manually, you can click the Send/Receive button any time you want. When you receive mail, there are two ways to read it. You can click the message once and read it in the Mail window, or you can double-click it to open the message in its own window. I think it's best to simply click the email once; that way, you don't have multiple open windows that you need to deal with.

ALERT: Email is received in the inbox. If Inbox is not selected, you must select it first.

1 Click the Send/Receive button.

2 Click the email message once.

3 View the contents of the email.

HOT TIP: You can adjust the size of the email panes by dragging the grey border between any of them up or down.

4 If you can't see the pictures in the email (if there are any), click the yellow bar.

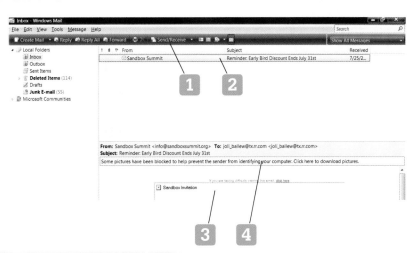

ALERT: Click to view pictures only if you know the sender. If you view the pictures in a spam message, the spammer will know your email address works and probably send you more spam.

ALERT: Before you can send and receive email using Outlook Express or Windows Mail, you have to set up an account using the instructions provided by your ISP.

WHAT DOES THIS MEAN?

Inbox: This folder holds mail you've received.

Outbox: This folder holds mail you've written but have not yet sent.

Sent items: This folder stores copies of messages you've sent.

Deleted items: This folder holds mail you've deleted.

Drafts: This folder holds messages you've started and saved, but not completed. Click File and then Save to put an email in progress here.

Junk email: This folder holds email that Windows Mail thinks is spam. You should check this folder occasionally, since Mail may put email in there that you actually want to read.

Spam: Junk email, unwanted email and sales ads.

Microsoft Communities: This folder offers access to available Microsoft newsgroups and communities.

View an attachment

An attachment is a file that you can send with an email, such as a picture, document or video clip. If an email that you receive contains an attachment, you'll see a paperclip. To open the attachment, click the paperclip icon in the Preview pane, and then click the attachment's name.

1 Click the email once in the Message pane.

2 Click the paperclip in the Preview pane.

3 Click the name of the attachment.

4 Click Open.

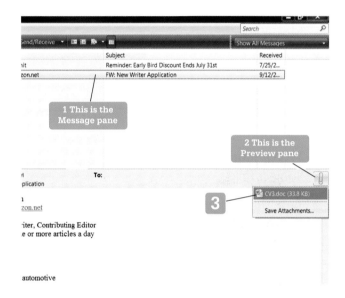

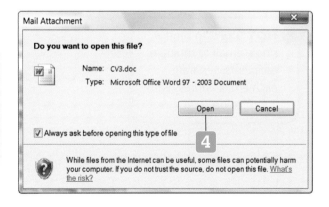

 ALERT: Hackers send attachments that look like they are from legitimate companies, banks and online services. Do not open these unless you are absolutely positive they're from a company you trust.

 ALERT: Attachments can contain viruses. Never open an attachment from someone you don't know.

 HOT TIP: Never open an attachment that ends in .zip unless you are sure it is from someone you trust and that it is not a virus.

Reply to an email

When someone sends you an email, you may need to send a reply back to them. You do that by selecting the email and then clicking the Reply button.

1. Select the email you want to reply to in the Message pane.

2. Click Reply.

3. In the To: field, type the email address for the recipient.

4. Type a subject in the Subject field.

5. Type the message in the body pane.

6. Click Send.

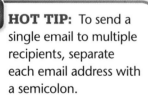

HOT TIP: To send a single email to multiple recipients, separate each email address with a semicolon.

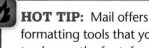

ALERT: If the email you are replying to was sent to you along with additional people, clicking Reply will send a reply to the person who composed the message. Clicking Reply To All will send the reply to everyone who received the email.

HOT TIP: Mail offers formatting tools that you can use to change the font, font colour, font size and more.

Forward an email

When someone sends you an email that you want to share with others, you forward the email by selecting the email and then clicking the Forward button.

1 Select the email that you want to forward in the Message pane.

2 Click Forward.

3 In the To: field, type the email address for the recipient.

4 Type a subject in the Subject field.

5 Type the message in the body pane.

6 Click Send.

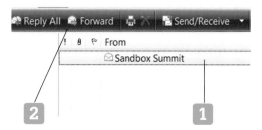

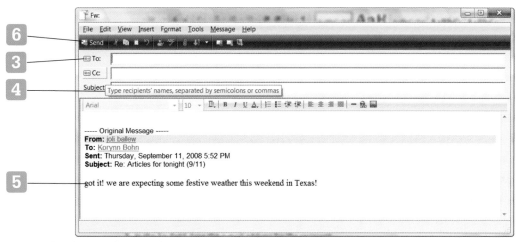

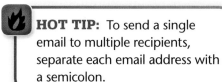

HOT TIP: To send a single email to multiple recipients, separate each email address with a semicolon.

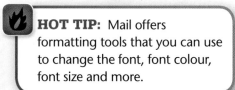

HOT TIP: Mail offers formatting tools that you can use to change the font, font colour, font size and more.

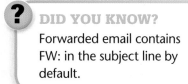

DID YOU KNOW?
Forwarded email contains FW: in the subject line by default.

Compose and send a new email

You compose an email message by clicking Create Mail on the toolbar. You input who the email should be sent to, and the subject, and then type the message.

1 Click Create Mail.

2 Type the recipient's email address in the To: line. If you want to add additional names, separate each email address with a semicolon.

3 Type a subject in the Subject field.

4 Type the message in the body pane.

5 Click Send.

? DID YOU KNOW?

In Mail there's a menu bar and a toolbar, which you can use to access other features, including tools you're already familiar with, such as cut, copy, paste, spell check, font, font size, font colour and font style.

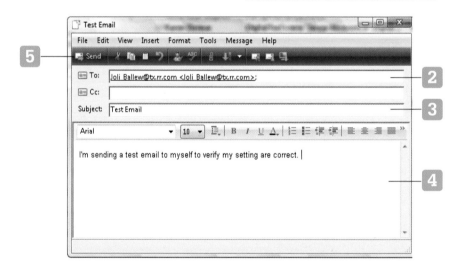

🔥 HOT TIP: Select Tools, and then click Select Recipients to add email addresses from your address book.

🔥 HOT TIP: Make sure the subject adequately describes the body of your email. Your recipients should be able to review the subject line later and be able to recall what the email was about.

? DID YOU KNOW?

If you want to send the email to someone and you don't need them to respond, you can put them in the CC line.

Attach a picture to an email using Insert

Although email that contains only text serves its purpose quite a bit of the time, often you'll want to send a photograph, a short video, a sound recording, a document or other data. When you want to add something to your message other than text, it's called adding an attachment. There are many ways to attach something to an email. One way is to use the Insert menu, and then choose File Attachment. Then you can browse to the location of the attachment and click Insert.

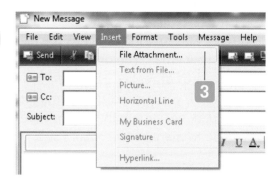

1 Click Create Mail.

2 Click Insert.

3 Click File Attachment.

4 If the item you want to attach is saved in your Documents folder, skip to step 6.

5 If the item you want to attach is not in the Documents folder, browse to the location of the folder.

6 Click the item you want to add and select Open.

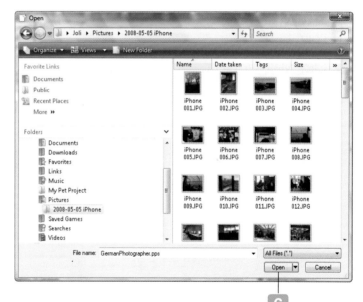

 HOT TIP: When inserting (adding) files to an email, hold down the Ctrl key to select non-contiguous files, and hold down the Shift key to select contiguous files.

? **DID YOU KNOW?**
If you can locate the file you want to attach, then you can drag the file to the email in progress.

! **ALERT:** Anything you attach won't be removed from your computer; instead, a copy will be created for the attachment.

Attach a picture to an email using right-click

You can create an email that contains an attachment by right-clicking the file you want to attach. This method attaches the files to a new email, which is fine if you want to create a new email. The only problem with this is that it doesn't work if you'd rather send forwards or replies. However, this method has a feature other methods don't: with this method, you can resize any images you've selected before sending them. This is a great perk because many pictures are too large to send via email, and resizing them helps you to manage the email's size.

1 Locate the file you'd like to attach and right-click it.

2 Point to Send To:.

3 Click Mail Recipient.

4 If the item you're attaching is a picture, choose the picture size.

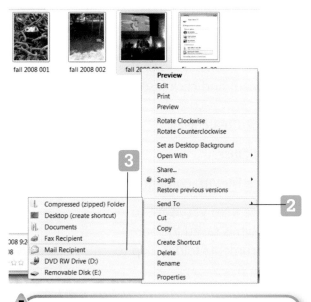

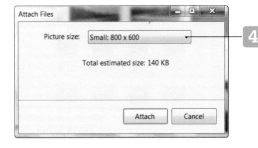

> ![] **ALERT:** Avoid sending large attachments, especially to people that you know have a dial-up modem or who get email only on a small device such as a BlackBerry, iPhone or mobile PC.

? DID YOU KNOW?
800 × 600 is usually the best option when sending pictures via email.

? DID YOU KNOW?
You can email from within applications, such as Microsoft Word and Excel. Generally, you'll find the desired option under the File menu, as a submenu of Send.

Add a contact

A contact is a data file that holds the information you keep about a person. The contact information looks like a contact card, and the information can include a picture, email address, mailing address, first and last name, and similar data. By default, Windows Mail creates a contact for each person you email; the data include the email address. You don't need to do anything to the contacts that Windows Mail creates unless you want to add data.

1 From Windows Mail, click the Contact icon on the toolbar.

2 Click New Contact.

3 Type all of the information you want to add.
Be sure to add information to each tab.

4 Click OK.

? DID YOU KNOW?

When someone gives you their email address and other personal data, you can create a contact card for them. From the File menu, select New, and then select Contact.

🔥 HOT TIP: Your contacts are stored in your Contacts folder inside your personal folder.

Print an email

Sometimes you'll need to print an email or its attachment. Windows Mail makes it easy to print. Just click the printer icon on the toolbar. After clicking the Print icon, the Print dialogue box will appear, where you can select a printer, set print preferences, choose a page range and print.

 Select the email you want to print by clicking the message in the Message pane.

 Click the Print icon.

3 In the Print dialogue box, select the printer you want to use, if more than one exists.

4 Click Print.

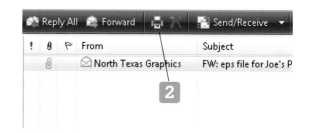

HOT TIP: A printer icon should appear on the right side of the taskbar during the print task. Click the icon for more information.

HOT TIP: You can configure print preferences and choose what pages to print using Preferences. Refer to your printer's user manual to find out what print options your printer supports.

Change how often Mail checks for email

You may want to have Mail check for email more or less often than every 30 minutes. It's easy to make the change.

1 Click Tools.

2 Click Options.

3 Click the General tab.

4 Change the number of minutes from 30 to something else.

5 Click OK.

? DID YOU KNOW?

You can change other settings in Mail from the other tabs in the Options dialogue box.

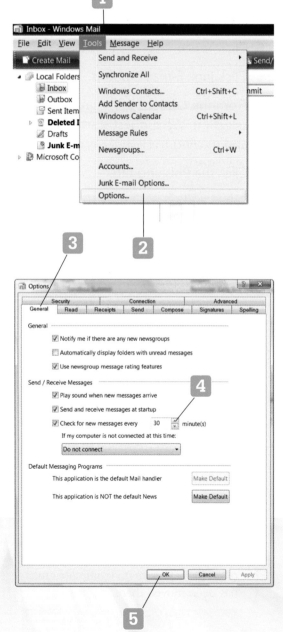

Apply a junk email filter

Just as you receive unwanted information from telephone marketers, radio stations and television ads, you're going to get unwanted advertisements in emails. This is referred to as junk email or spam. Most of these advertisements are scams and rip-offs, and some contain pornographic images. There are four filtering options in Windows Mail: No automatic filtering, Low, High, and Safe List Only.

1 Click Tools

2 Click Junk E-mail Options.

3 From the Options tab, make your selection. We suggest starting at Low and moving to High if necessary later.

4 Click the Phishing tab.

5 Select Protect my Inbox from messages with potential Phishing links. Additionally, move phishing email to the Junk Email folder.

6 Click OK.

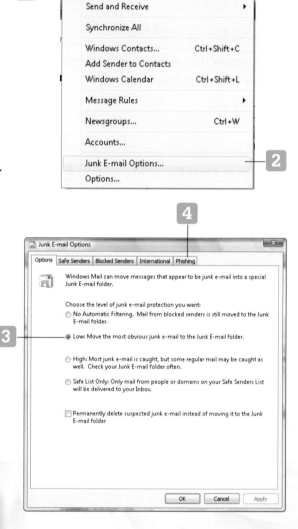

ALERT: Don't give your email address to any website or company, or include it in any registration card, unless you're willing to receive junk email from them and their constituents.

ALERT: Check the junk email folder often to make sure no legitimate email has been moved there.

WHAT DOES THIS MEAN?

No Automatic Filtering: Use this only if you do not want Windows Mail to block junk email messages. Windows Mail will continue to block messages from email addresses listed on the Blocked Senders list.

Low: Use this option if you receive very little junk email. You can start here and increase the filter if it becomes necessary.

High: Use this option if you receive a lot of junk email and want to block as much of it as possible. Use this option for children's email accounts. Note that some valid email messages will probably be blocked, so you'll have to review your junk email folder occasionally to make sure you aren't missing any email that you want to keep.

Safe List Only: Use this option if you only want to receive messages from people or domain names on your Safe Senders list. This is a drastic step and requires that you add every sender you want to receive mail from to the Safe Senders list. Use this as a last resort.

ALERT: Never buy anything from a junk email, send money to a sick or dying person who you don't know, send money for your portion of a lottery ticket or fall for any other spam hoaxes.

Create a folder

It's important to perform some housekeeping chores once a month or so. If you don't, Windows Mail may become bogged down and perform slower than it should, or you may be unable to manage the email you want to keep. One way to keep Mail under control is to create a new folder to hold email that you want to keep and then move mail into it.

1 Right-click Local Folders.

2 Select New Folder.

3 Type a name for the new folder.

4 Select Local Folders.

5 Click OK.

6 Note the new folder in the Local Folders list.

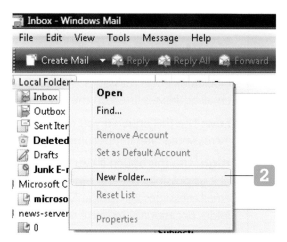

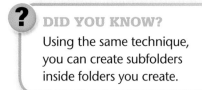

DID YOU KNOW?

Using the same technique, you can create subfolders inside folders you create.

HOT TIP: Name folders descriptively, such as Funny Jokes, Receipts and Pictures.

Move email to a folder

Moving an email from one folder (such as your inbox) to another (such as Funny Jokes) is a simple task. Just drag the email from one folder to the other.

1 Right-click the email message you want to move in the message pane. Then hold down the mouse button while dragging the message to the new folder.

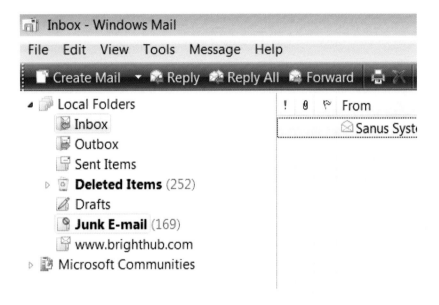

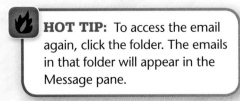

HOT TIP: To access the email again, click the folder. The emails in that folder will appear in the Message pane.

Delete email in a folder

In order to keep Mail from getting bogged down, you'll need to delete email in folders. Depending on how much email you get, this may be as often as once a week.

1 Right-click Junk Email.

2 Click Empty 'Junk Email' Folder.

3 Right-click Deleted Items.

4 Click Empty 'Deleted Items' Folder.

HOT TIP: Select any email in any folder, and click the red X to delete it.

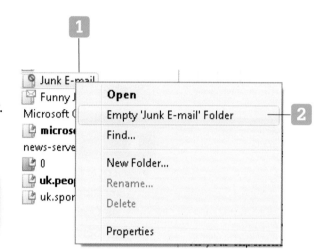

9 Stay secure

Introduction

Both Windows Vista and Windows XP come with a lot of built-in features to keep you and your computer safe. These security tools help to protect you from all kinds of danger, including online predators and unscrupulous co-workers. It's important that you enable these features and heed any security warnings when they are given in order to fully protect you, your PC and your data.

Add a new user account

You created an administrator user account when you first turned on your PC. This account defines your personal folders and holds your settings for your Desktop background, screen saver and other items, and gives you control over your PC and its settings. If you share your PC with someone else, they should have their own user account too, but it should be a standard or limited account.

1 Click Start.

2 Click Control Panel.

3 Click Add or remove user accounts.

4 Click Create new account.

5 Type a new account name.

6 Verify that Standard user is selected.

ALERT: If every person who accesses your PC has their own standard user account and password, and if every person logs on using that account and then logs off the PC each time they've finished using it, then you'll never have to worry about anyone accessing anyone else's personal data.

7 Click Create Account.

8 Click the X in the top right corner to close the window.

 DID YOU KNOW?
Administrators can make changes to system-wide settings, but Standard users cannot, without an Administrator name and password.

ALERT: All accounts should have a password applied to them.

 HOT TIP: You can also click Change the picture, Change the account name, Remove the password, and other options to further personalise the account.

Require a password

All user accounts, even yours, should be password-protected. When a password is configured, you must type the password to gain access to the computer. This protects the PC from unauthorised access.

1 Click Start.

2 Click Control Panel.

3 Add or remove user accounts.

4 Click the user account that you want to apply a password to.

5 Click Create password.

6 Type the new password, type it again to confirm it, and type a password hint.

7 Click Create password.

8 Click the X in the top right of the window to close it.

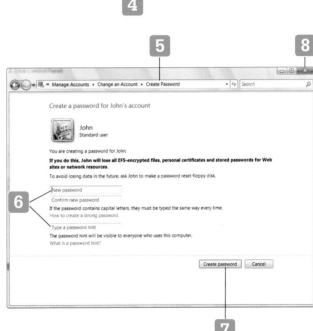

John
Standard user

4

5   **8**

Create a password for John's account

John
Standard user

You are creating a password for John.

If you do this, John will lose all EFS-encrypted files, personal certificates and stored passwords for Web sites or network resources.

To avoid losing data in the future, ask John to make a password reset floppy disk.

6

New password

Confirm new password

If the password contains capital letters, they must be typed the same way every time.

How to create a strong password

Type a password hint

The password hint will be visible to everyone who uses this computer.

What is a password hint?

Create password   Cancel

7

 DID YOU KNOW?
When you need to make a system-wide change, you have to be logged on as an administrator or type an administrator's user name and password.

ALERT: Create a password that contains upper- and lower-case letters and a few numbers. Write the password down and keep it somewhere out of sight and safe.

HOT TIP: You can also click Change the picture, Change the account name, Remove the password, and other options to further personalise the account.

Configure Windows Update

It's very important to configure Windows Update to get and install updates automatically. This is the easiest way to ensure that your computer is as up-to-date as possible, at least as far as patching security flaws that Microsoft uncovers, having access to the latest features, and obtaining updates to the operating system itself. I suggest that you verify that the recommended settings are enabled as detailed here and then check occasionally for optional updates manually.

1 Click Start.

2 Click Control Panel.

3 Click Security.

4 Click Windows Update.

5 In the left pane, click Change Settings.

6 Configure the settings as shown here, and click OK.

Security
Check for updates
Check this computer's security status
Allow a program through Windows Firewall

Windows Update
Turn automatic updating on or off | Check for updates | View installed updates

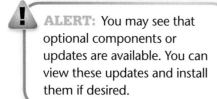

ALERT: You may see that optional components or updates are available. You can view these updates and install them if desired.

? **DID YOU KNOW?**

If the computer is not online at 3.00 a.m., then it will check for updates the next time it is.

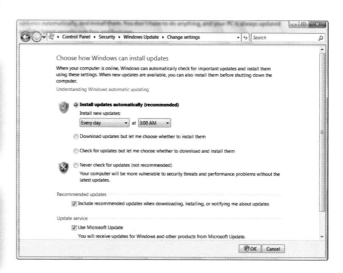

WHAT DOES THIS MEAN?

Windows Update: If enabled and configured properly, when you are online Vista will check for security updates automatically and then install them. You don't have to do anything, and your PC is always updated with the latest security patches and features.

Scan for viruses with Windows Defender

You don't have to do much to Windows Defender except understand that it offers protection against Internet threats such as malware. It's enabled by default and it runs in the background. However, if you ever think your computer has been attacked by an Internet threat (e.g. virus, worm, malware), you can run a manual scan here.

1 Click Start.

2 Click Control Panel.

3 Click Security.

4 Click Windows Defender.

 Windows Defender
Scan for spyware and other potentially unwanted software

5 Click the arrow next to Scan (not the Scan icon). Click Full Scan if you think the computer has been infected.

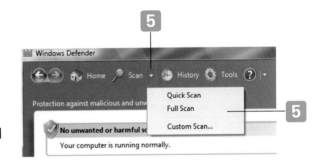

6 If a virus is detected, follow the prompts to quarantine the infected files.

7 Click the X in the top right corner to close the Windows Defender window.

WHAT DOES THIS MEAN?

Malware: Malicious software, such as viruses, worms and spyware.

Enable the firewall

Windows Firewall is a software program that checks the data that come in from the Internet and local networks and then decides whether the data are good or bad. If the firewall deems the data harmless, it will allow the data to come though the firewall; if not, the data are blocked.

1 Click Start.

2 Click Control Panel.

3 Click Security.

4 Under Windows Firewall, click Turn Windows Firewall on or off.

5 Verify that the firewall is on. If not, select On.

6 Click OK.

ALERT: You have to have a firewall to keep hackers from gaining access to your PC, and to help prevent your computer from sending out malicious code if it is ever attacked by a virus or worm.

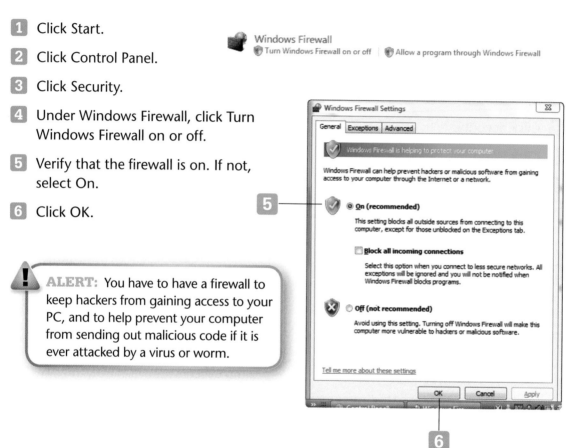

Windows Firewall
Turn Windows Firewall on or off | Allow a program through Windows Firewall

Windows Firewall Settings

General | Exceptions | Advanced

Windows Firewall is helping to protect your computer

Windows Firewall can help prevent hackers or malicious software from gaining access to your computer through the Internet or a network.

On (recommended)

This setting blocks all outside sources from connecting to this computer, except for those unblocked on the Exceptions tab.

Block all incoming connections

Select this option when you connect to less secure networks. All exceptions will be ignored and you will not be notified when Windows Firewall blocks programs.

Off (not recommended)

Avoid using this setting. Turning off Windows Firewall will make this computer more vulnerable to hackers or malicious software.

Tell me more about these settings

OK | Cancel | Apply

View and resolve Security Center warnings

The Security Center is a talkative application. You'll see a pop-up if your antivirus software is out-of-date or not installed, if you don't have the proper security settings configured, or if Windows Update or the firewall is disabled. You'll also get a user account control prompt each time you want to install a program or make system-wide changes.

> **ALERT:** When you see alerts such as this, pay attention! You'll want to resolve them.

> **? DID YOU KNOW?**
> Vista comes with malware protection but not antivirus protection.

 1 Click Start.

2 Click Control Panel.

3 Click Security.

4 If there's anything in red or yellow, click the down arrow, if necessary, to see the problem.

5 Note the resolution and perform the task.

6 Continue in this manner to resolve all Security Center-related issues.

 7 Click the X in the top right corner of the Security Center window to close it.

> **ALERT:** Install antivirus software to protect your PC from viruses and worms.

WHAT DOES THIS MEAN?

Virus: A self-replicating program that infects computers with intent to do harm. Viruses often come in the form of attachments in emails.

Worm: A self-replicating program that infects computers with intent to do harm. However, unlike a virus, it does not need to attach itself to a running program.

10 Digital pictures

Introduction

Of all of the ways people use their computers, working with digital pictures is right up there with surfing the Internet and sending email in terms of popularity. There's nothing quite as exciting as taking a digital picture with your digital camera, saving it to your PC and then emailing it to friends and family. It's just as cool to be able to edit the picture and print it. Windows XP and Windows Vista both offer applications for viewing and managing digital pictures. Vista's application is called Photo Gallery, which is what I discuss here.

Install a printer

As with installing a camera, to install a printer you insert the CD that came with the printer, plug in the printer and turn it on, and wait for the computer to install it.

 ALERT: It's usually best to connect the new printer, turn it on and then let Vista or XP install it. You need to intervene only if Vista or XP can't install the printer on its own.

 DID YOU KNOW?
When you install everything on the CD that comes with your printer, you're probably installing applications you'll never use and don't need.

 ALERT: Read the directions that come with each new device you acquire. If there are specific instructions for installing the driver on a Vista or XP PC, follow those directions rather than the generic directions offered here.

1️⃣ Connect the printer to a wall outlet.

2️⃣ Connect the printer to the PC using either a USB cable or a parallel port cable.

3️⃣ Insert the CD for the device, if you have it.

4️⃣ If a pop-up message appears regarding the CD, click the X to close the window.

5️⃣ Turn on the device.

6️⃣ Wait while the driver is installed.

 DID YOU KNOW?
Leave the CD in the drive. If Vista wants any of the information on the CD, it will acquire it from there.

 DID YOU KNOW?
USB is a faster connection than a parallel port, but FireWire is faster than both.

Install a digital camera or webcam

Most of the time, adding a camera is as simple as inserting the CD that came with the camera, plugging in the new hardware and turning it on, and waiting for the computer to install it. However, it's always best to have directions for performing a task, so in that vein I've included them here.

1 Read the directions that came with the camera. If there are specific instructions for installing the driver, follow them. If not, continue here.

2 Connect the camera to a wall outlet or insert fresh batteries.

3 Connect the camera to the PC using either a USB cable or a FireWire cable.

4 Insert the CD for the device, if you have it.

5 If a pop-up message appears, click the X to close the window.

6 Turn on the camera. Place it in Playback mode if that exists. Often, simply turning on the camera is enough.

7 Wait while the driver is installed.

ALERT: It's usually best to connect the new camera, turn it on and then let Vista or XP install it. You need to intervene only if the computer can't install the hardware on its own.

? DID YOU KNOW?
When you install everything on the CD that comes with your camera, you're probably installing applications you'll never use and don't need.

5

WHAT DOES THIS MEAN?

Driver: Software that allows the PC and the new hardware to communicate with each other.

USB: A technology used to connect hardware to a PC. A USB cable is often used to connect a digital camera to a PC.

FireWire: A technology used to connect hardware to a PC. A FireWire cable is often used to connect a digital video camera to a PC.

 ALERT: If the camera does not install properly, refer to the camera's user manual.

 DID YOU KNOW?

Even if you aren't installing the CD, leave the CD in the drive. If Vista wants any of the information on the CD, it will acquire it.

Open Photo Gallery and view a picture

You can use pictures in a lot of different ways with Vista, but Windows Photo Gallery is the best. With this, you have easy access to slideshows, editing tools and picture groupings. You can sort, filter and organise as desired.

1 Click Start.

2 Type Photo Gallery in the Start Search window.

3 From the Start results, under Programs click Windows Photo Gallery.

WHAT DOES THIS MEAN?

View pane: The pane to the left is the View pane, where you select the folder or subfolder that contains the pictures you want to view, manage, edit or share.

Expand a tree: Click the right-facing arrow to show the contents of a folder.

Thumbnail pane: The pane on the right, where you preview the pictures in the folder selected in the View pane.

? **DID YOU KNOW?**

You can click Start, and then All Programs, and then Windows Photo Gallery.

? **DID YOU KNOW?**

Your digital pictures are stored in the Pictures folder on your hard drive, not in or by Photo Gallery. Photo Gallery offers a place to view and work with images and has nothing to do with how they are stored on the PC.

4 In the View pane, expand the Folders tree and then the Pictures tree.

5 Select any folder name.

6 Hover the mouse over any picture to see a larger thumbnail of the picture.

7 Click Pictures at the top of the View window.

8 Click the X to close Windows Photo Gallery.

Upload digital photos

After you've taken pictures with your digital camera, you'll want to move or copy those pictures to the computer. Once stored on the computer's hard drive, you can view, edit, email and print the pictures.

1 Connect the device. If applicable, turn it on.

2 When prompted, choose Import Pictures using Windows.

3 Type a descriptive name for the group of pictures you're importing.

4 Click Import.

? DID YOU KNOW?
These steps also work for importing pictures from a mobile phone.

HOT TIP: If desired, tick Erase after importing. This will cause Vista to erase the images from the device after the import is complete.

ALERT: If your device isn't recognised when you plug it in and turn it on, in Windows Photo Gallery click File, and then click Import from Camera or Scanner.

► SEE ALSO: Installing a digital camera is covered earlier in this chapter.

Import pictures from a media card

If your digital camera has a media card, and your computer has a built-in media card reader, you can insert the card into the reader and import your pictures. You do not have to connect the camera or turn it on.

1 Remove the media card from the camera and insert it into the media card reader.

2 When prompted, choose Import Pictures using Windows.

3 Type a descriptive name for the group of pictures you're importing.

4 Click Import.

 DID YOU KNOW?

Some printers come with media card readers built right in. If you have such a printer, and it's turned on, you can insert the card there.

HOT TIP: If desired, tick Erase after importing. This will cause Vista to erase the images from the device after the import is complete.

WHAT DOES THIS MEAN?

Media card: A small, thin card (usually 3cm by 2cm) that holds data in digital devices such as cameras.

Media card reader: A slot usually in the side of a laptop or at the front of a PC or printer that allows you to insert a media card and retrieve the information on it.

View a slideshow of pictures

This allows you to view pictures in a folder in full screen and have them move from one to the other automatically, and view a slideshow of the picture.

1 Open Windows Photo Gallery.

2 Expand any folder that contains pictures.

3 Click the Play Slide Show button. Wait at least three seconds.

4 To end the show, press the Esc key on the keyboard.

HOT TIP: Press the F11 key on the keyboard to start a slideshow.

Auto adjust picture quality

With pictures now on your computer and available in Windows Photo Gallery, you can perform some editing. Photo Gallery offers you the ability to correct brightness and contrast, tint and saturation, among other things.

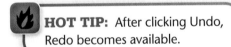
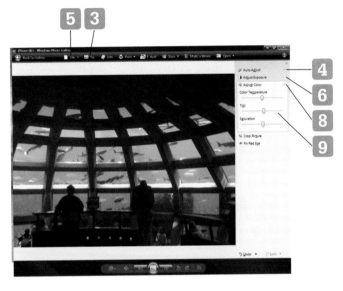
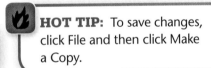

1 Open Photo Gallery.

2 Double-click a picture to edit.

3 Click Fix.

4 Click Auto Adjust.

5 If you do not like the result, click File and click Undo.

6 Click Adjust Exposure.

7 Move the sliders for brightness and contrast. Click Revert to return to the original image settings.

8 Click Adjust Colour.

9 Move the sliders for colour temperature, tint and saturation. Click Revert to return to the original image settings.

> **HOT TIP:** After clicking Undo, Redo becomes available.

> **HOT TIP:** To save changes, click File and then click Make a Copy.

> **ALERT:** Click Back to Gallery to return to the picture gallery (the previous screen).

WHAT DOES THIS MEAN?

Auto Adjust: This tool automatically assesses the image and alters it, which, most of the time, results in a better image. However, there's always the Undo button, and you'll probably use it on occasion.

Adjust Exposure: This tool offers slider controls for brightness and contrast. You move these sliders to the left and right to adjust as desired.

Adjust Color: This tool offers slider controls to adjust the temperature, tint and saturation of the photo. Temperature runs from blue to yellow, allowing you to change the atmosphere of the image. Tint runs from green to red, and saturation moves from black and white to colour.

Fix red eye

The Fix Red Eye tool lets you draw a rectangle around any eye that has a red dot in it in a photo to remove the red dot.

1 Open Photo Gallery.

2 Double-click a picture to edit.

3 Click Fix.

4 Click Fix Red Eye.

5 Drag the mouse over the red part of the eye. When you let go, the red eye in the picture will be removed.

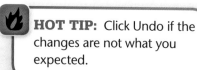 **HOT TIP:** Click Undo if the changes are not what you expected.

WHAT DOES THIS MEAN?

Red eye: The result of a flash reflecting in the eyes of the subject.

Crop a picture

To crop means to remove parts of a picture that you don't want by repositioning the picture and removing extraneous parts. You can also rotate the frame.

1 Open Photo Gallery.

2 Select the picture that you want to crop.

3 Click Fix.

4 Click Crop Picture.

5 Drag the corners of the box to resize it, and drag the entire box to move it around in the picture.

6 Click Apply.

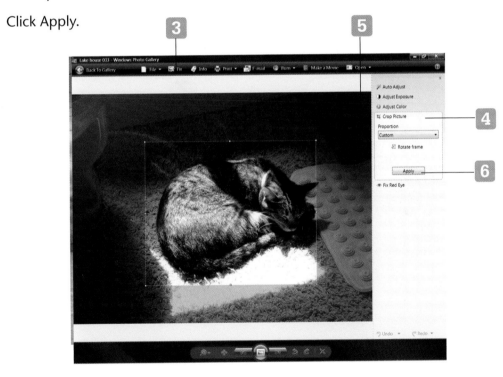

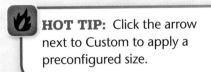

HOT TIP: Click the arrow next to Custom to apply a preconfigured size.

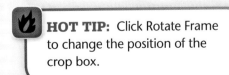

HOT TIP: Click Rotate Frame to change the position of the crop box.

Email a picture

You can email photos that you want to share from inside Photo Gallery. You can also choose the size to email them; I suggest you use either small or medium for best results.

 1 Open Windows Photo Gallery.

2 Select the pictures you want to email.

3 Click E-mail.

4 Select a picture size.

5 Click Attach.

6 Compose the email and send it.

HOT TIP: For email, generally 800 × 600 is best. It's small enough to be sent and received quickly, even on dial-up connections, and it fits nicely in the recipient's inbox.

 DID YOU KNOW?
The larger the image, the longer it will take to send and receive.

SEE ALSO: Composing and sending a new email is covered in Chapter 8.

Change the size of a thumbnail

When previewing images in Photo Gallery, you view the image's thumbnail. A thumbnail is a miniature version of the picture. You can change the size of the thumbnail using the slider at the bottom.

1 Open Photo Gallery.

2 Click the icon at the bottom that looks like a magnifying glass.

3 Move the slider to change the thumbnail's size.

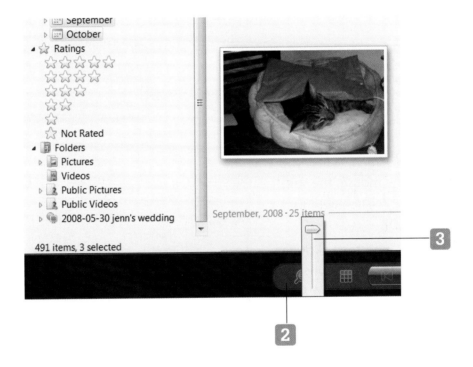

Take a screen shot

The Snipping Tool lets you drag your mouse cursor around any area on the screen to copy and capture it. Once you've captured the area, you can save it, edit it and send it to an email recipient. You can write on the picture with a red, blue, black or customised pen or a highlighter, and if you mess up you can use the eraser.

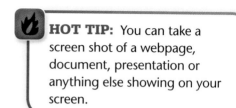

HOT TIP: You can take a screen shot of a webpage, document, presentation or anything else showing on your screen.

1 Click Start.

2 In the Start Search dialogue box, type Snip.

3 Under Programs, select Snipping Tool.

4 Drag your mouse across any part of the screen. When you let go of the mouse, the snip will appear in the Snipping Tool window.

5 Click Tools, and then click Pen to access the pen options. You can use the pen to draw on the snip.

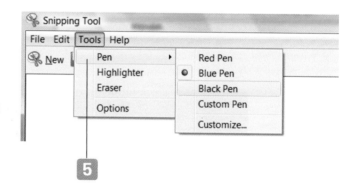

HOT TIP: If you mess up, from the Tools menu choose Eraser and then erase the mistake.

ALERT: If you want to keep the snip, you have to save it. Click File and then click Save As to name the file and save it to your hard drive.

Email a screen shot

You can use the Snipping Tool to take a picture of your screen as detailed in the previous section. You can write on the screen shot with a 'pen' and email the screen shot if you'd like to share it with someone.

1 Take a screen shot with the Snipping Tool.

2 Click File, and then click Send To.

3 Click E-mail Recipient.

4 Insert the recipient's name, change the subject if desired, type a message if desired, and then click Send.

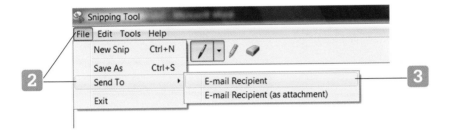

HOT TIP: Emails that you have sent can be viewed in Mail's Sent folder.

ALERT: If you select Email Recipient, this will insert the snip inside an email. Note that you can also send the snip as an attachment.

11 Music, DVDs and Windows Media Player

Introduction

Windows Media Player comes with Windows XP and Windows Vista. If you have Windows XP, you can upgrade Media Player to the version included with Windows Vista if you want to. Windows Media Player offers all you need to manage your music library, get music online and copy the CDs from your music collection to your computer. You can also use Media Player to burn music CDs share music using your local network, watch DVDs and more.

Open Media Player

You open Media Player in the same way that you open other programs, from the Start menu. Once opened, you'll need to know where the Category button is, so you can access different kinds of media. We'll start with music.

1 Click Start.

2 Type Media Player.

3 Under Programs, click Windows Media Player to open it.

4 Click the arrow next to the Category button.

5 Click Music.

ALERT: The version of Media Player used in this chapter is Media Player 11, the version that comes with Vista. To upgrade, visit **www.microsoft.com**

? DID YOU KNOW?
By default, Music is selected.

ALERT: The first time you start Windows Media Player 11, you'll be prompted to set it up. Choose Express to accept the default settings.

? DID YOU KNOW?
You can select Pictures, Video and other options to access different types of media.

Listen to a song

To play any music track, simply navigate to the track and double-click it. Songs are listed in the Navigation pane.

1 Open Media Player.

2 If necessary, click the Category button and choose Music.

3 Click Album. (Note you can also click Songs, Artist or any other category to locate a song.)

4 Double-click any album to play it.

> **SEE ALSO:**
> Opening Media Player is covered in the previous section.

? DID YOU KNOW?
Media Player has Back and Forward buttons, which you can use to navigate Media Player.

? DID YOU KNOW?
The controls at the bottom of the screen from left to right are: Shuffle (to play songs in random order), Repeat, Stop, Previous, Play/Pause, Next, Mute and a volume slider.

Copy a CD to your hard drive

You can copy CDs to your hard drive. This is called 'ripping'. Once music is on your computer, you can listen to it in Media Player, burn compilations of music to other CDs and put the music on a portable music player.

1 Insert the CD that you want to copy into the CD drive.

2 If any pop-up boxes appear, click the X to close them.

3 In Windows Media Player, click the Rip button.

4 Deselect any songs that you do not want to copy to your computer.

5 Click Start Rip.

HOT TIP: You can watch the rip progress in the List pane.

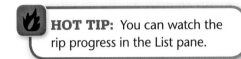

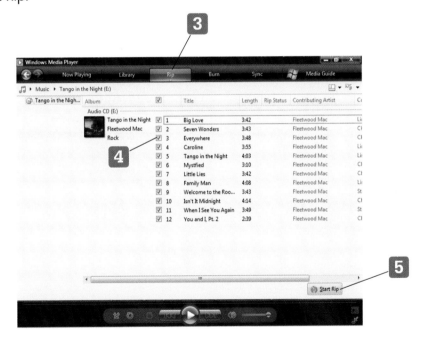

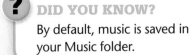

ALERT: When you insert a blank recordable CD, you may see pop-up boxes. Close them to rip a CD using the Windows Media Player interface.

DID YOU KNOW?

By default, music is saved in your Music folder.

Copy music files to a CD

There are two ways to take music with you when you are on the go. You can copy the music to your computer or a portable device such as a music player, or you can create your own CDs, choosing the songs to copy and placing them on the CD in the desired order.

1 Open Media Player.

2 Click the arrow under the Burn tab.

3 Verify that Audio CD has a dot by it. If it does not, click it once.

4 Verify that Apply Volume Leveling Across Tracks on Audio CDs has a tick by it.

5 Click outside the drop-down list to close it.

? DID YOU KNOW?

Media Player will keep track of the songs you select and will let you know when you're running out of space on the CD you're creating.

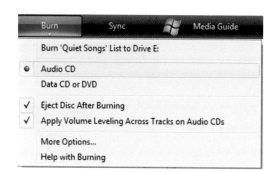

| Burn | Sync | Media Guide |

Burn 'Quiet Songs' List to Drive E:

● Audio CD

Data CD or DVD

✓ Eject Disc After Burning
✓ Apply Volume Leveling Across Tracks on Audio CDs

More Options...

Help with Burning

 ALERT: A typical CD can hold about 80 minutes of music.

? DID YOU KNOW?

CDs that you create in Media Player can be played in car stereos, portable CD players and other CD devices.

6 Insert a blank CD in the CD drive, and close any pop-up dialogue boxes.

7 Under Library, click Songs or Album.

8 Click any song title or album that you want to add, and then drag it to the List pane.

9 When you've added the songs you want, click Start Burn.

CD R

39:28 remaining

Burn List ▼ ✕

Current Disc

Big Love - Fleetwood Mac	3:41
Tango in the Night	4:02
Circle Dance - Bonnie Raitt	4:11
Distance - Karsh Kale	5:27
Love Comes - The Posies	3:19
I Guess You're Right	3:32
Love Comes - The Posies	3:19
I Guess You're Right	3:32
Cool Clear Water - Bonnie...	5:27
Dimming of the Day	3:39

Quiet Songs

🔥 Start Burn

9

Quiet Songs
Aisha Duo

Tango in the Night
Fleetwood Mac

Paste Art Here

Unknown

DID YOU KNOW?

Look at the slider in the List pane to see how much room is left on the CD.

DID YOU KNOW?

You can right-click any entry to access additional options, including Remove from List, Move Up and Move Down.

HOT TIP: You can drag and drop playlists too. There is more information on playlists later in this chapter.

WHAT DOES THIS MEAN?

Burn: A term used to describe the process of copying music from a computer to a CD.

Volume levelling: Makes all songs on the CD record at the same volume, so that some tracks are not louder or softer than others.

Create a playlist

Playlists allow you to organise songs the way you like to listen to them. You might consider creating playlists that contain songs specific to an occasion, such as a dinner party or wedding. Then, when the event happens, you can simply start the playlist and let the music take care of itself.

1 Open Windows Media Player.

2 Click Create Playlist.

3 When you click Create Playlist, the text will turn blue. Type the name of the playlist here.

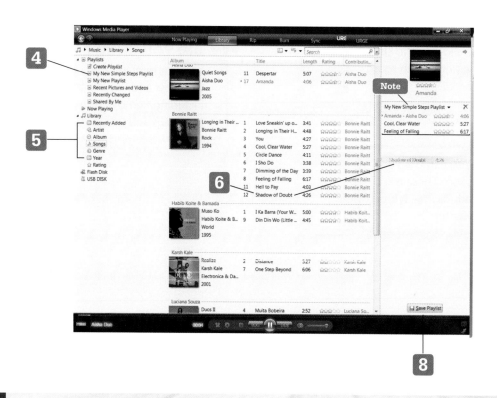

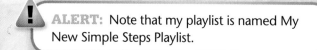

ALERT: Note that my playlist is named My New Simple Steps Playlist.

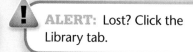

ALERT: Lost? Click the Library tab.

4 The new playlist name will appear under Playlists. Click the name. When you click the new playlist, it will appear in the List pane.

5 Click Recently Added, Artist, Album, Songs, Genre and Year as needed to locate the songs that you want to add to the playlist.

6 Drag those songs to the Playlist Pane.

7 Continue to drag and drop songs.

8 When finished, click Save Playlist.

? DID YOU KNOW?

To play any playlist, double-click it in the Playlists pane in the Navigation Windows.

Shadow of Doubt	☆☆☆☆☆	4:26
Seven Wonders - Flee...	☆☆☆☆☆	3:43
Mystfied - Fleetwood ...	☆☆☆☆☆	3:10
Little Lies - Fleetwood...	☆☆☆☆☆	3:41
I Ka Barra (Your Work..	☆☆☆☆☆	5:00
Din Din Wo (Little Chi...	☆☆☆☆☆	4:45
Distance - Karsh Kale	☆☆☆☆☆	5:27
One Step Beyond	☆☆☆☆☆	6:06
Symphony No. 3 in E-...	☆☆☆☆☆	5:56
I Guess You're Right	☆☆☆☆☆	3:32
Love Comes - The Pos...	☆☆☆☆☆	3:19

8

Create an auto playlist

You can create an auto playlist by sorting media you have by criteria that you set, such as the year a song or album was released, the speed of the song or the date you last played the song.

1 Open Windows Media Player.

2 Right-click Playlists.

3 Select Create Auto Playlist.

4 Type a name for the playlist.

5 Under Music in my library, click [Click here to add criteria]. (This will disappear when you click it and you'll see what's shown here.)

6 From the drop-down list, select your criteria.

7 After making your selection, look for a criterion that needs to be set. Click it to configure it.

8 Continue to add criteria as desired.

9 When you are finished, click OK.

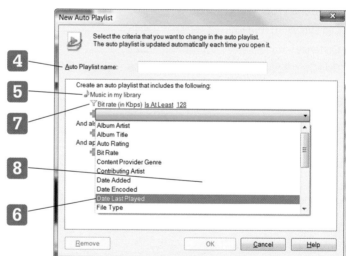

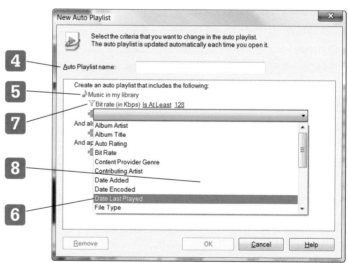

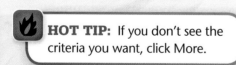

HOT TIP: If you don't see the criteria you want, click More.

Share your music

If you have more than one computer in your home and you network them to each other, you can share your media library between them. Sharing allows you to keep only one copy of your media, such as music, videos and pictures, on just one PC, while sharing it with other computers, media extenders and Microsoft's Xbox 360.

1 Open Windows Media Player.

2 Click the arrow under Library.

3 Select More Options.

4 Verify that the Library tab is selected. Click Configure Sharing.

5 Click Share My Media. Click OK.

6 Select Other users of this PC.

7 Click Allow.

8 Click Settings to verify the defaults. Click OK.

9 Click OK twice more.

ALERT: After clicking Share My Media and clicking OK, the screen will look like this:

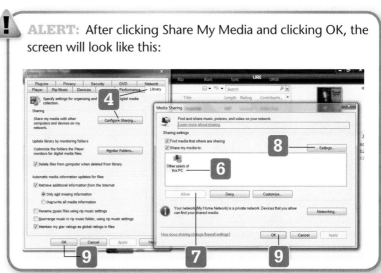

? DID YOU KNOW?

The default settings are fine, but if you want to make changes, such as not allowing pictures to be shared, you can do that here.

! ALERT: The Vista computer that stores the media you want to share must be connected to your home network. The network must be private.

Watch a DVD

You can watch a DVD on your computer just as you would on any DVD player. Vista offers two choices for doing so, Windows Media Center and Windows Media Player. We'll talk about Windows Media Player here.

1 Find the button on the computer that opens the DVD drive door. Press the button.

2 Place the DVD in the door and press the button again to close it.

3 When prompted, choose Play DVD movie using Windows Media Player.

? DID YOU KNOW?
If you have Windows Vista Home Premium or Vista Ultimate, you have Windows Media Center. It's best to watch DVDs in Media Center, if you have it, rather than Media Player.

SEE ALSO: If the DVD plays automatically and no choice is offered, refer to the section Change AutoPlay settings in Chapter 12.

HOT TIP: The controls you'll see and use in Media Player are very similar to, and perhaps exactly the same as, the controls on your own DVD player.

12 Change system defaults

Introduction

Vista comes preconfigured with certain settings called system defaults. These include things such as how folders look on the screen and the date and time. You can make changes to these defaults and other settings and what shows on the taskbar.

Change AutoPlay settings

Your computer doesn't know what you want it to do when you insert a blank CD, a DVD movie or a music CD, so most of the time it asks you by offering a dialogue box. You can tell Vista what you want it to do when you insert or access media though, thus bypassing the prompt and getting right to the music, picture or DVD that you want to play or view.

1 Click Start.

2 Click Default Programs on the Start menu.

3 Click Change AutoPlay settings.

4 Use the drop-down lists to select the program that you want to use for the media you want to play.

5 Click Save.

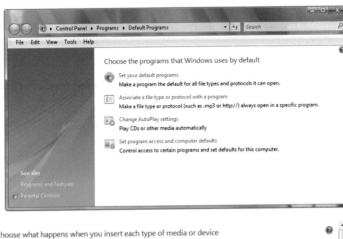

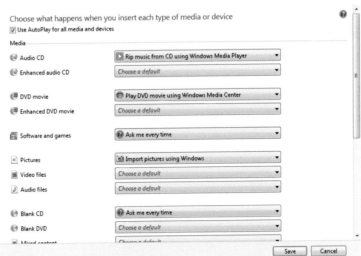

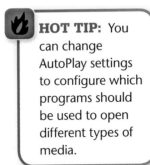

HOT TIP: You can change AutoPlay settings to configure which programs should be used to open different types of media.

HOT TIP: For audio CDs, choose Rip music from CD using Windows Media Player.

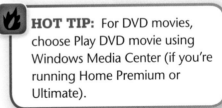

HOT TIP: For DVD movies, choose Play DVD movie using Windows Media Center (if you're running Home Premium or Ultimate).

Change the date and time

If you have a laptop, you'll probably want to change the date and time, or at least the time zone, when you travel. You can do this from the Date and Time dialogue box.

1 Click Start.

2 Click Control Panel.

3 Click Clock, Language and Region.

4 Click Set the time and date.

5 Click Change date and time.

6 Use the arrows or type in a new time.

7 Select a new date.

8 Click OK.

9 Click OK.

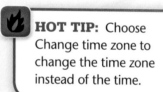

HOT TIP: Choose Change time zone to change the time zone instead of the time.

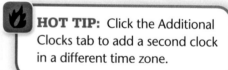

HOT TIP: Click the Additional Clocks tab to add a second clock in a different time zone.

Change language settings

If you speak and work in multiple languages, you may want to change keyboards or other input methods. You can do this from Control Panel.

 Click Start.

2 Click Control Panel.

3 Click Clock, Language, and Region.

4 Click Regional and Language Options.

5 Make changes as desired from the available drop-down lists.

6 Click OK.

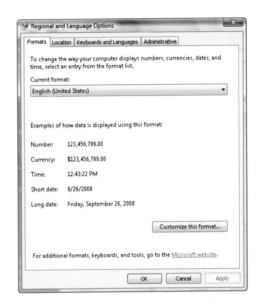

 DID YOU KNOW?

You can customise any format by clicking the Customise this format button.

HOT TIP: To set your current location, click the Current Location tab and select the desired country from the drop-down list.

Change folder options

You can change how folders react by configuring Folder Options. You can single-click instead of double-clicking to open a folder, choose to open each folder in its own window, view hidden files and folders, and more.

1 Click Start.

2 In the Start Search window, type Folder Options.

3 Under Programs in the results list, click Folder Options.

4 From the General tab, read the options and make changes as desired.

5 From the View tab, read the options and make changes as desired.

6 From the Search tab, read the options and make changes as desired.

HOT TIP: If you're more comfortable with older operating systems, choose Use Windows Classic folders.

HOT TIP: Select Always show menus and every folder will offer menus where available.

HOT TIP: To shorten the list of search results, deselect Find partial matches.

Change touchpad and mouse settings

The speed the cursor moves on the screen when you use the touchpad or mouse, the shape of the cursor and other settings can all be changed from their defaults. You can change the settings, perhaps turning a right-handed touchpad into a left-handed touchpad, using Mouse settings.

1 Click Start, and in the Start Search window type mouse.

2 In the results, under Programs click Mouse Properties.

3 From the Buttons tab, read the options and make changes as desired.

4 From the Pointers tab, select a theme as desired (as shown here).

5 From the Pointer Options tab, read the options and make changes as desired.

6 From the Wheel tab, read the options and make changes as desired.

7 Click OK.

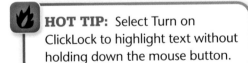 **HOT TIP:** Select Turn on ClickLock to highlight text without holding down the mouse button.

 HOT TIP: Just for fun, try the Dinosaur theme. When the computer is busy, the mouse pointer will look like a dinosaur instead of the default moving blue circle.

 HOT TIP: If you're not happy with how fast the pointer moves when you move your mouse, you can change the speed here.

HOT TIP: Enable Snap To and the mouse will move to the default option in dialogue boxes.

Enable Quick Launch

Quick Launch is an area of the taskbar where you can access programs quickly. You can put any program's icon there, including icons for third-party programs that you use often.

1 Right-click an empty area of the taskbar.

2 Click Properties.

3 From the Taskbar tab, read the options and click Show Quick Launch.

4 Click OK.

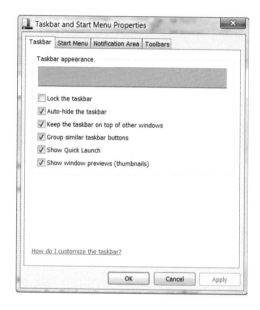

HOT TIP: To keep the taskbar hidden when you aren't using it, click Auto-hide the taskbar.

WHAT DOES THIS MEAN?

Taskbar: The grey screen that runs across the bottom of your desktop.

Add icons to the Quick Launch area of the taskbar

Once it is enabled, the Quick Launch area offers you a place to access programs that you use often. You can place program icons there by dragging them from the All Programs menu.

1 Click Start.

2 Click All Programs.

3 Locate the program that you'd like to add a shortcut to in Quick Launch.

4 Drag the item to the Quick Launch area and drop it there.

 **DID YOU KNOW?**
This process will not remove the item from the All Programs list.

 HOT TIP: You'll see the program's icon, as shown here, during the dragging process.

13 Share data and printers

Introduction

Both Windows Vista and Windows XP let you share data and printers with other computers on your network. However, you must turn on these features, because by default sharing is not enabled. Once you've turned on sharing, you can save data to the Public folder, share a personal folder, and view and manage your shared data.

Sharing data and printers in Vista differs greatly from sharing data and printers in Windows XP. If you have Windows XP, try right-clicking the item that you want to share. Usually, you'll find a Sharing option or a Properties option in the menu that appears, and you can use that to configure sharing. This chapter gives details on Vista.

Open the Network and Sharing Center

The Network and Sharing Center is where you tell Vista what you want to share with others on your network.

1 Click Start.

2 In the Start Search window, type Network and Sharing.

3 Under Programs, click Network and Sharing Center.

4 The Network and Sharing Center opens.

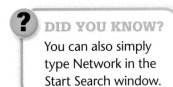

DID YOU KNOW?
You can also simply type Network in the Start Search window.

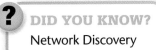

DID YOU KNOW?
Network Discovery must be turned on in order for your PC to find other PCs and to share data.

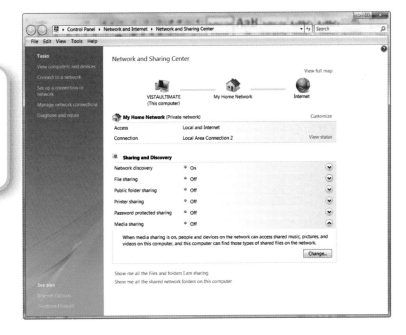

ALERT: Notice the down arrows in the list. Clicking these arrows reveals more information about each section.

Turn on file sharing

When you turn on file sharing, data that you have shared are accessible by other users on your local network.

1 Open the Network and Sharing Center.

2 Click the down arrow by File sharing.

3 Click Turn on file sharing.

4 Click Apply.

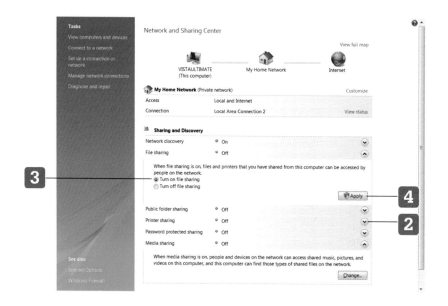

Turn on printer sharing

When you turn on printer sharing, printers that you have shared are accessible by other users on your local network. You must turn on printer sharing in order for other PCs to obtain access to your shared printers.

1 Open the Network and Sharing Center.

2 Click the down arrow by Printer sharing.

3 Click Turn on printer sharing.

4 Click Apply.

HOT TIP: Click Start, and in the Start Search window type Printers. You can then open the Printers folder to manage shared printers.

SEE ALSO: Sharing a printer is covered in the next section.

Share a printer

After turning on printer sharing, you'll need to manually share the printer(s) you want other users to have access to.

1 Click Start, and in the Start Search window type Printers.

2 Under Programs, click Printers.

3 Locate the printer you want to share.

4 Right-click the printer, and then click Sharing.

5 Click Share this printer.

6 Click OK.

> ⚠ **ALERT:** Your PC and printer will need to be turned on in order for others to access the shared printer.

> ⚠ **ALERT:** When other users on your network access the printer for the first time, they may be prompted to install a driver for it. This is OK and will be managed by the PC.

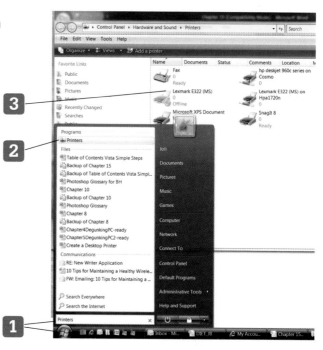

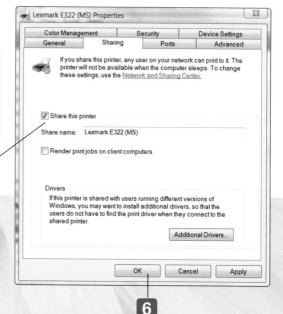

Turn on Public folder sharing

When you turn on Public folder sharing, data that you have saved in the Public folders will be accessible by other users on your local network. You must turn on Public folder sharing in order for other PCs to obtain access to the Public folders on your PC.

1 Open the Network and Sharing Center.

2 Click the down arrow by Public folder sharing.

3 Make a sharing selection.

4 Click Apply.

ALERT: If you turned on file sharing earlier, Public folder sharing will already be enabled. However, follow these steps to view and change the sharing settings.

? DID YOU KNOW?
Selecting the middle choice as shown here allows users to access, read and change the data inside the Public folders.

Turn on password-protected sharing

When password-protected sharing is on, only people who have a user account and a password on the computer can access shared files and printers. If you want all users to input a user name and password, enable this feature.

1 Open the Network and Sharing Center.

2 Click the down arrow by Password-protected sharing.

3 Click Turn on password protected sharing and click Apply.

ALERT: Users who have a user name but not a password will not be able to access files until they apply a password to their account.

ALERT: This feature does not have to be turned on in order to share files and folders.

Turn on media sharing

Media includes photos, music, videos and other things. Media sharing must be turned on in order to share media with others on your network.

1 Open the Network and Sharing Center.

2 Click the down arrow by Media Sharing.

3 Click Change.

4 Click Share my media.

5 Click OK.

6 Set the sharing options and click OK.

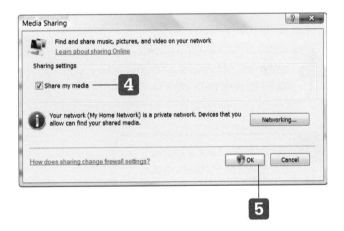

Save data to the Public folder

If you've enabled Public folder sharing, you'll want to save data to share in the Public folders.

1 Open a picture, document or other item that you wish to save to the Pubic folders.

2 Click File, and click Save As.

3 In the Save As dialogue box, click Public.

4 Select the Public subfolder that you want to save to.

5 Type a name for the file.

6 Click Save.

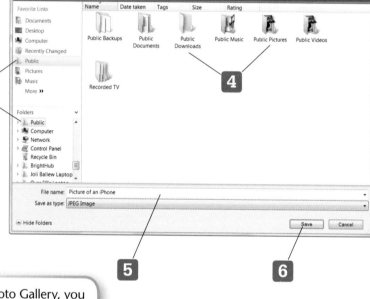

ALERT: In Windows Photo Gallery, you click File and then click Make a Copy.

HOT TIP: Save pictures to the Public Pictures folder. Save documents to the Public Documents folder.

SEE ALSO: Moving a file is covered in Chapter 4.

DID YOU KNOW?
It's actually better to move data that you want to share into the Public folders. That way, you won't create duplicate copies of the data on your hard drive.

Access the Public folder

You can access the Public folder by browsing to it. This may require you to browse the network if the Public folders are stored on another PC.

1 Click Start, and then click your user name.

2 Use the scroll bars in the left pane to locate Public.

3 Click Public.

4 Double-click the Public folder to open it.

? **DID YOU KNOW?**

You can drag data from other open folders here to copy or move data. Remember to right-click while dragging.

Share a personal folder

Sometimes you won't want to move or copy data into Public folders and subfolders. Instead, you'll want to share data directly from your own personal folders. To do this, you'll have to share the desired personal folders.

1 Locate the folder to share.

2 Right-click the folder.

3 Choose Share.

4 Click the down arrow shown here, and select any user (or Everyone) to share the folder with.

5 Click Add.

6 Click the arrow next to the new user name.

7 Select a sharing option.

8 Click Share.

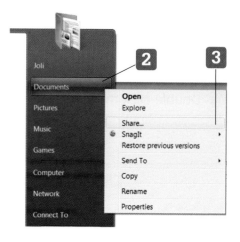

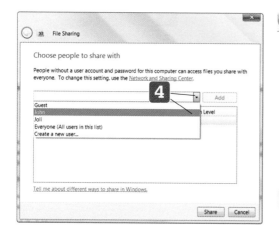

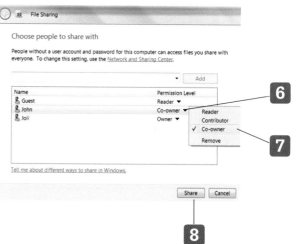

WHAT DOES THIS MEAN?

Owner: This is the person who created the file, uploaded the picture, purchased or ripped the music, or saved the video.

Co-owner: This is a person who has owner permissions and who can edit, delete and add files to the folder.

Reader: This person can only access, not edit, what's in the folder.

14 Use Help and Support

Introduction

You will sometimes need help outside of this book. When this happens, you can count on the Help and Support Center in Windows XP and Windows Vista. You can access the Help and Support Center from the Start menu. In addition to general help and support, you can access specific help from any application included with Windows Vista, such as Mail and Internet Explorer. Finally, you can usually click Help in a third-party application if you need assistance.

Open Help and Support

Help and Support is located on the Start menu.

1 Click Start.

2 Click Help and Support.

3 Click any item in Help and Support to drill down into the help topics.

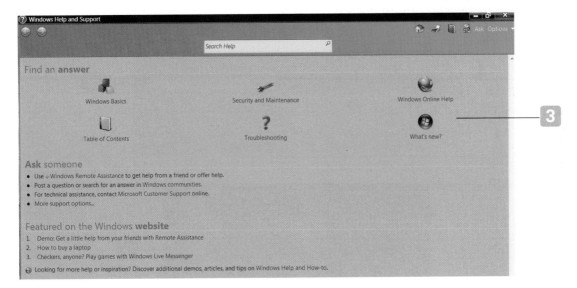

Search Help

If you don't see what you're looking for on the Windows Help and Support welcome page, you can search for the answers you need.

1 Think of a word or short phrase that describes the problem or the item you'd like more information on.

2 Type that word or phrase into the Search Help window.

3 Press Enter on the keyboard.

4 Choose the desired option from the results.

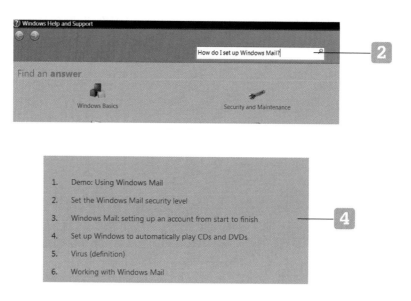

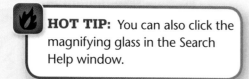 **HOT TIP:** You can also click the magnifying glass in the Search Help window.

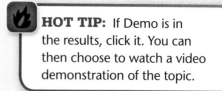 **HOT TIP:** If Demo is in the results, click it. You can then choose to watch a video demonstration of the topic.

Browse Help

Sometimes you can't find what you want by searching for it. You may be interested in learning about a topic or want to explore options for maintaining, securing or customising your PC. In these cases, you may want to browse for help.

1 Open Help and Support.

2 Click the arrow by Options.

3 Browse Help.

4 Click any topic heading to learn more about the item listed.

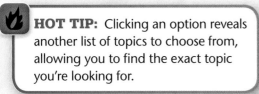

HOT TIP: Clicking an option reveals another list of topics to choose from, allowing you to find the exact topic you're looking for.

Get help online

You can go on the Internet to get more help and to access help topics written after you purchased your PC. To do this, click the Windows Online Help option from Help and Support's Home page.

1 Click the Home icon to return to the Help and Support Center's Home page.

2 Click Windows Online Help.

3 Click any topic icon to learn more and to access the help and support articles.

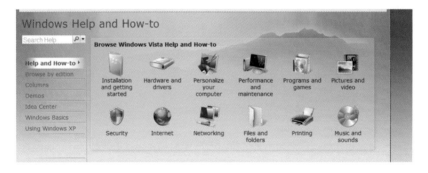

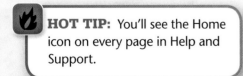 **HOT TIP:** You'll see the Home icon on every page in Help and Support.

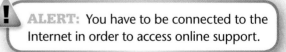 **ALERT:** You have to be connected to the Internet in order to access online support.

Get help from a dialogue box

A dialogue box is, technically, a box that does not have any option to minimise, restore or maximise it. You can see a dialogue box here. The only option in the corner is to close it by clicking the X. Dialogue boxes almost always contain a link to an appropriate help page.

1 When in a dialogue box, look for a link to a help topic.

2 Click that link to access the associated help page.

189

? DID YOU KNOW?

Dialogue box help links take you to the Help and Support Center, and usually not to an online help page.

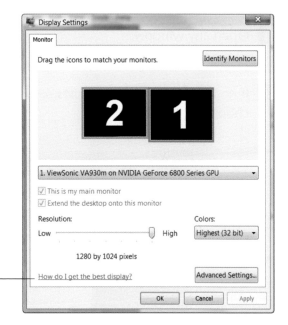

Access help from an open window

A window is, technically, a box or rectangle that contains options to minimise, restore and maximise it. Windows almost always offer a link to support. Accessing support requires you to click the blue question mark or click the Help option on the menu bar.

1 Open any window.

2 Locate the blue question mark if one is available, and then click it.

3 If no blue question mark exists, look for a Help option on the menu bar. Click it and choose View Help.

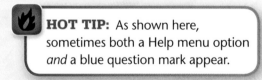

HOT TIP: As shown here, sometimes both a Help menu option *and* a blue question mark appear.

Access Mail's Help feature

Windows Mail comes with its own help pages. As with any window, you can access Help and Support from the Help menu.

1 Open Windows Mail.

2 Click Help.

3 Click View Help.

4 Browse through the Help topics to find the information you need.

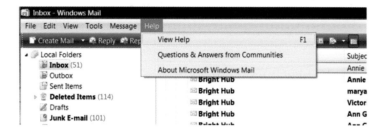

? DID YOU KNOW?

There's no blue question mark in Windows Mail for accessing Help and Support.

Access Internet Explorer's Help feature

Internet Explorer offers help in a variety of ways. You can click the blue question mark on the Command bar or click the Alt key to access the menu bar. You can also access help from a variety of dialogue boxes.

1 Open Internet Explorer.

2 If you can see the blue question mark icon on the Command bar, click it to access help.

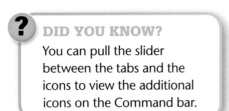

3 If you cannot see the blue question mark, click the arrow shown here to access it.

4 You can also click the Alt key on the keyboard to make the menu bar appear, and then access Help from there.

? DID YOU KNOW?
You can pull the slider between the tabs and the icons to view the additional icons on the Command bar.

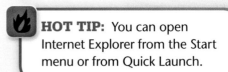

HOT TIP: You can open Internet Explorer from the Start menu or from Quick Launch.

Access Windows Update Help and Support feature

Windows Update, like several other Windows features, offers multiple help options.

1 Open Windows Update.

2 Click Help on the menu bar to access the help pages.

3 Click the blue question mark to access the help pages.

4 Click any 'learn' option to access help.

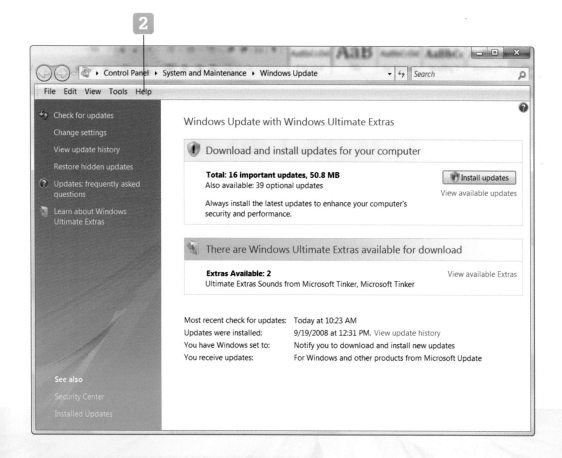

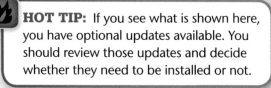

HOT TIP: If you see what is shown here, you have optional updates available. You should review those updates and decide whether they need to be installed or not.

Access help from a third-party program

Almost all applications come with a help centre. To open the help pages, you can click F1 on the keyboard or look for the Help menu.

1 Open any program.

2 Look for a help menu.

3 Look for a blue question mark.

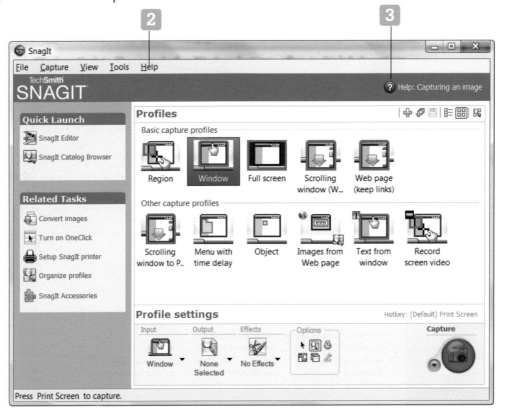

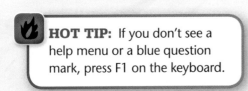

HOT TIP: If you don't see a help menu or a blue question mark, press F1 on the keyboard.

15 Improve computer performance

Introduction

There are lots of ways to improve your computer's performance. You can disable unnecessary programs, adjust visual effects and turn off WiFi. You can also install antivirus software and change your power settings. In this chapter we'll explore all of this and more.

Use Windows Defender to disable unnecessary programs

Windows Defender offers protection against Internet threats such as malware. It's enabled by default and it runs in the background. You can also use Windows Defender to disable unnecessary programs that you need to keep but don't need to run in the background.

1 Click Start.

2 Click Control Panel.

3 Click Security.

4 Click Windows Defender.

5 Click Tools.

6 Click Software Explorer.

7 Select a program from the list that you want to disable.

8 Click Disable.

9 Close Windows Defender.

? DID YOU KNOW?
You can also click Start and type Windows Defender in the Start Search window to access the program.

! ALERT: When you click Disable, the program will not start when you boot the PC. It will start once you click it, though. This does not uninstall the program.

Adjust visual effects

If your computer runs slowly or if you have a laptop and you'd like to extend the battery life, you can adjust visual effects for best performance.

1 Click Start.

2 In the Start Search window, type System.

3 Click System in the results.

4 In the System window, click Advanced System Settings.

5 Click Settings under Performance.

6 Change from the default to Adjust to best performance.

7 Click OK.

8 Click OK.

9 Close the System window.

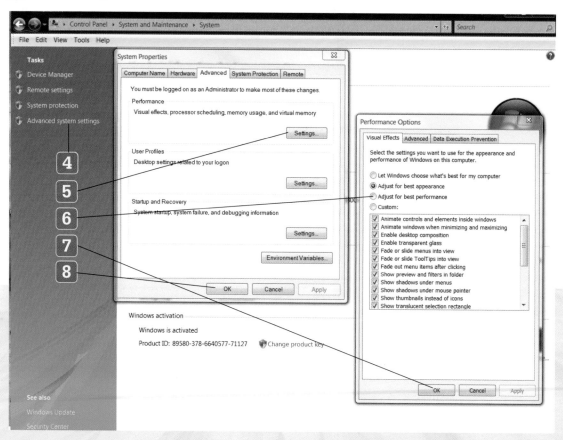

Adjust indexing options

Vista indexes the files stored on your computer. By indexing these files, Vista is able to offer search results more quickly than without indexing because, instead of looking through every file on the hard drive, it simply looks to the index, finds the location of the file and then goes right to it.

1 Click Start.

2 In the Start Search window, type Performance.

3 Click Performance Information and Tools in the results.

4 In the Performance Information and Tools window, click Adjust indexing options.

5 Note the data that are indexed. If you see anything other than data that you use often, click it and then click Modify.

6 Deselect the unwanted item and click OK.

7 Click Close to close the Indexing dialogue box.

? DID YOU KNOW?

If you tell Windows to index all of the files on your PC, your searches will actually slow down. You want Vista to index your personal files and folders but nothing else.

! ALERT: Continue to index users, your email program and the Start menu.

View battery life and change battery status

From the Battery Status window in Windows Mobility Center, you can see how much life is left in your battery's current charge. You can also change the power plan currently used here.

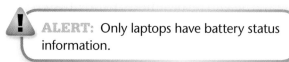

ALERT: Only laptops have battery status information.

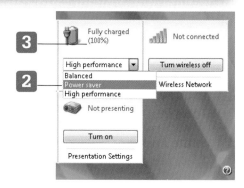

1 Open Mobility Center.

2 Click the arrow to view the three power plans: Balanced, Power saver, and High performance. Pick one.

3 View the current status of the battery life.

HOT TIP: The easiest way to conserve battery power and improve battery life is to use the Power Saver plan, available in Windows Mobility Center (among other places).

? DID YOU KNOW?
There is a battery meter icon on the taskbar. It looks like a power meter and plug. To see the status of the battery, hover the mouse over the icon.

WHAT DOES THIS MEAN?

Balanced: This is the default power plan. You won't get the best power savings with this plan, and you won't get the best performance either.

Power Saver: This plan is all about lengthening battery life. That means in all instances, even when the laptop is plugged in, you'll be able to notice decreased brightness and processor levels, and the computer will go to sleep, turn off hard disks and turn off the display within minutes of inactivity.

High Performance: This power plan doesn't worry about battery life. Here, Vista provides 100 per cent of your CPU's processing power, which is necessary for playing games and performing resource-intensive tasks.

Turn on and off WiFi

You may want to turn off WiFi to increase battery life or if you are travelling and are told to do so by an airline pilot. This applies only to laptops.

1 Open Mobility Center.

2 Click Turn wireless off to disable WiFi.

3 Click Turn wireless on to enable it.

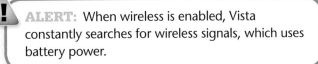

ALERT: When wireless is enabled, Vista constantly searches for wireless signals, which uses battery power.

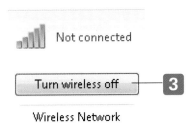

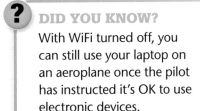

DID YOU KNOW?

With WiFi turned off, you can still use your laptop on an aeroplane once the pilot has instructed it's OK to use electronic devices.

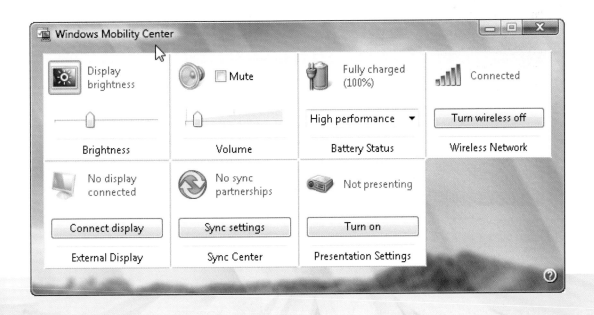

Change when the computer sleeps

You can change how much time elapses before the computer goes to sleep. The less idle time configured, the more battery power and electricity you'll save.

1 Open Mobility Center.

2 In the Battery Status window, click the battery icon.

3 Click Change when the computer sleeps.

4 Edit the plan settings to the desired configuration, and then click Save Changes.

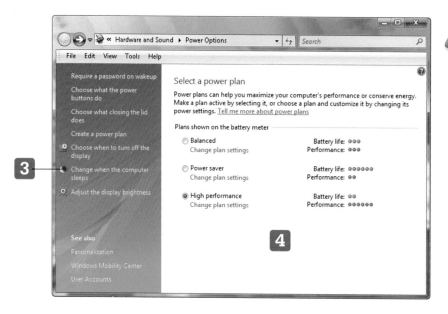

ALERT: The Mobility Center is available only in laptops.

HOT TIP: You can change the power plan on a desktop PC too. Just click Start, and in the Start Search window type Power.

HOT TIP: To learn more about power plans, click Tell me more about power plans in the Power Options window.

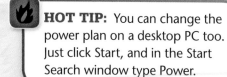
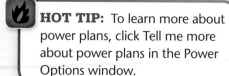

Change what happens when you press the power button

You can change what happens when you press the power button on a PC or laptop or close the laptop's lid. You can choose from Shut down, Do nothing, Sleep and Hibernate.

1 Click Start.

2 In the Start Search window, type Power.

3 Choose Power options.

4 Click Choose what the power buttons do.

5 Edit the plan settings to the desired configuration, and then click Save Changes.

6 Click Save Changes.

7 Close the window.

Know your Windows Experience Base Score

Your Windows Experience Base Score gives you an idea of how well your computer performs. You can use this score and its related information to improve the performance of your PC by adding memory and performing other upgrades.

1 Click Start.

2 In the Start Search dialogue box, type Performance.

3 From the results, click Performance Information and Tools.

4 Note the base score.

5 Click What do these numbers mean? to learn more about the numbers you see.

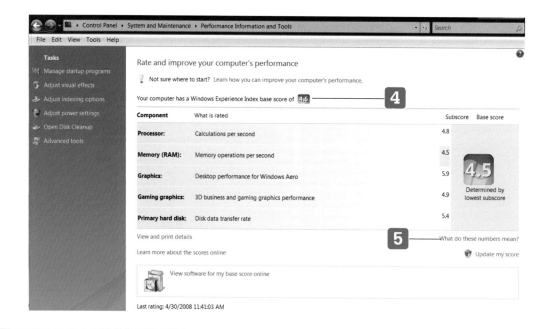

Install antivirus software

Windows XP and Windows Vista do not come with preinstalled antivirus software. You have to install that yourself.

1 Purchase antivirus software.

2 Follow the instructions for installation.

3 Configure the software to protect your PC from email and Internet threats, and to scan regularly for viruses.

4 Configure the software to download updates nightly.

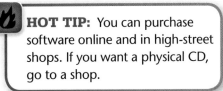

HOT TIP: You can purchase software online and in high-street shops. If you want a physical CD, go to a shop.

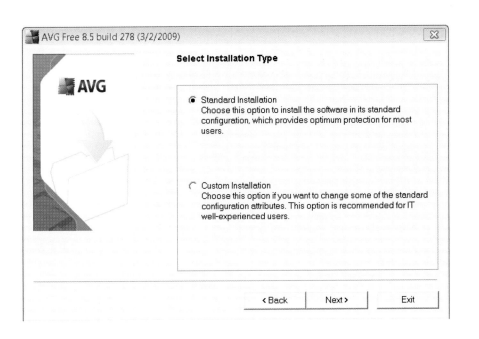

16 Fix problems

Introduction

When problems arise, you will probably want to resolve them quickly. Vista offers plenty of help. System Restore can fix problems automatically by restoring your computer to a time when it was working properly. If the boot-up process is slow, you can disable unwanted startup items. When you can't connect to the Internet, you can use the Network and Sharing Center to help you resolve the problem. You can use Device Manager to roll back a driver that didn't work, and if your computer seems bogged down you can delete unwanted programs and files easily. To keep your computer running smoothly, you can also apply some routine maintenance with Disk Cleanup and Disk Defragmenter.

Enable System Restore

If enabled, System Restore regularly creates and saves restore points that contain information about your computer that Windows uses to work properly. If your computer starts acting oddly, you can use System Restore to restore your computer to a time when it was working properly.

1 Click Start.

2 In the Start Search box, type System Restore.

3 Click System Restore under the Programs results.

4 Click Open System Protection.

5 Verify that the C: drive, or the System drive, is selected. If it is not, select it.

6 Click OK.

7 In the System Restore window, click Cancel.

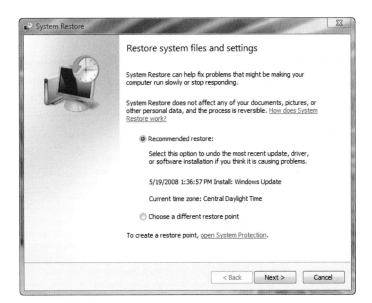

WHAT DOES THIS MEAN?

Restore point: A snapshot of the state of the system that can be used to make an unstable computer stable again.

 ALERT: System Restore can't be enabled unless the computer has at least 300 MB of free space on the hard disk, or if the disk is smaller than 1 GB.

Use System Restore

When a problem occurs on your computer, your first step to resolving the problem is often System Restore. Use System Restore when you download or install software or hardware that causes a problem for the computer, or whenever the computer seems unstable.

 Open System Restore.

 Click Next to accept and apply the recommended restore point.

 Click Finish.

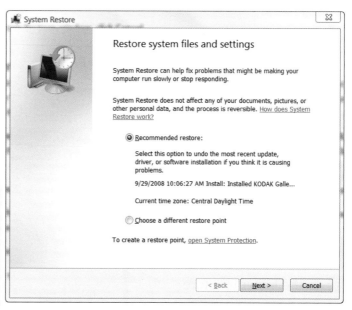

DID YOU KNOW?
Because System Restore works only with its own system files, running System Restore will not affect any of your personal data. Your pictures, email, documents music, etc. will not be deleted or changed.

DID YOU KNOW?
System Restore is a system utility. It can't recover a lost personal file, email or picture.

ALERT: If you're running System Restore on a laptop, make sure the laptop is plugged in. System Restore should never be interrupted.

ALERT: If you have a virus, System Restore probably won't work to resolve the problem, as viruses often attack personal files as well as system files.

Disable unwanted startup items

Lots of programs and applications start when you boot your computer. This causes the startup process to take longer than it should, and programs that start also run in the background, slowing down your computer's performance. You should disable unwanted startup items to improve all-round performance.

1 Click Start.

2 In the Start Search window, type System Configuration.

3 Under Programs, click System Configuration.

4 From the Startup tab, deselect third-party programs that you recognise but do not use daily.

5 Click OK.

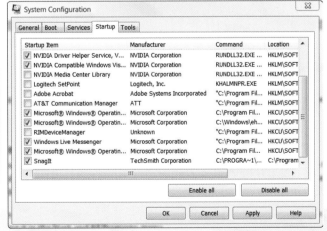

? DID YOU KNOW?

Even if you disable a program from starting when Windows does, you can still start the program when you need it by clicking it in the Start and All Programs menu.

! ALERT: You'll have to restart the computer in order to apply the changes.

! ALERT: Do not deselect anything you don't recognise or the operating system!

Resolve Internet connectivity problems

When you have a problem connecting to your local network or to the Internet, you can often resolve the problem in the Network and Sharing Center.

1 Open the Network and Sharing Center.

2 Click the red X.

3 Perform the steps in the order in which they are presented.

ALERT: You won't see a red X if the network is functioning properly.

Network and Sharing Center

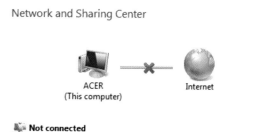

ACER
(This computer)

Internet

Not connected

? DID YOU KNOW?
Almost all of the time, performing the first step will resolve your network problem.

ALERT: If you're prompted to reset your broadband or satellite connection, turn off all hardware, including the computer, and then restart them in the following order: cable/satellite/DSL modem, router, computers.

2

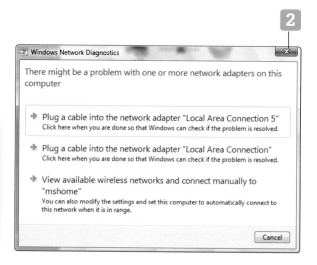

Windows Network Diagnostics

There might be a problem with one or more network adapters on this computer

→ Plug a cable into the network adapter "Local Area Connection 5"
Click here when you are done so that Windows can check if the problem is resolved.

→ Plug a cable into the network adapter "Local Area Connection"
Click here when you are done so that Windows can check if the problem is resolved.

→ View available wireless networks and connect manually to "mshome"
You can also modify the settings and set this computer to automatically connect to this network when it is in range.

Cancel

 ALERT: Make sure your cable modem, router, cables and other hardware are properly connected, plugged in and turned on.

Use Device Driver Rollback

If you download and install a new driver for a piece of hardware and it doesn't work properly, you can use Device Driver Rollback to return to the previously installed driver.

> **ALERT:** You can only roll back to the previous driver. This means that if you install a driver (D1) and it doesn't work, and then you install another driver (D2) and it doesn't work, using Device Driver Rollback will revert to D1, not the driver before it.

1. Click Start.

2. Right-click Computer.

3. Click Properties.

4. Under Tasks, click Device Manager (not shown).

5. Click the + sign next to the hardware that uses the driver to rollback.

6. Double-click the device name.

7. Click the Driver tab.

8. Click Rollback driver.

9. Click OK.

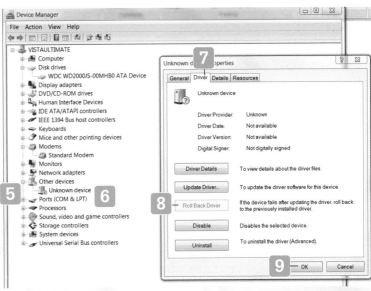

> **ALERT:** The Rollback driver option will be available only if a new driver has been installed recently.

> **ALERT:** You may have to restart your computer.

Reconnect loose cables

Many problems occur due to loose or disconnected cables. A mouse can't work unless it or its wireless component is plugged in. A cable modem can't work unless it's connected securely to the computer and the wall. When troubleshooting, always check your connections first.

1 Locate the hardware device that is not working.

2 Follow the cord to verify that it is connected to a power source, if required.

3 Follow any cables from the device to the computer to verify that the device is connected securely.

4 Restart the computer if the hardware does not begin to work within a few seconds.

 DID YOU KNOW?

Many pieces of hardware have multiple connections and connection types. If one type of connection doesn't work, such as USB, try another, such as FireWire, instead.

ALERT: If you aren't sure whether a cable is inserted properly, remove and then reinsert it.

View available hard drive space

Problems can occur if your hard drive space gets too low. This can become a problem when you use a computer to record television programmes or movies (these require a lot of hard drive space), or if your hard drive is partitioned.

1 Click Start.

2 Click Computer.

3 In the Computer window, click the C: drive.

4 View the available space.

 ALERT: If you find you are low on disk space, you'll have to delete unnecessary files and applications.

HOT TIP: If you see a second drive, as shown here, click it too; you may find that you can move data from the C: drive to the second drive to recover much needed space on the C: drive.

SEE ALSO: Moving and deleting files and folders is covered in Chapter 4.

WHAT DOES THIS MEAN?

Partition: Some hard drives are configured to have multiple sections, called partitions. The C: partition may have 20 GB available, while the D: partition may have 60 GB available. If you save everything to the C: partition but fail to ever use the D: partition, the C: partition can get full quickly.

Delete unwanted Media Center media

One of the places you'll find data hogging files is in Media Center's storage areas. This is especially true if you record television programmes or movies, or create your own movies. TV and movies take up a lot of hard drive space.

1 Open Media Center.

2 Under TV + Movies, click Recorded TV.

3 If folders exist, click the folder to open them.

4 Right-click any recordings and click Delete.

5 Repeat as necessary.

? DID YOU KNOW?
You can also find unwanted media in the Video and Pictures libraries.

HOT TIP: If you see that a series that you don't watch is recording, right-click it, choose Series Info and click Cancel Series.

WHAT DOES THIS MEAN?

Media Center: A feature included with Vista Home Premium and Vista Ultimate. You can use it to record and watch television, among other things.

Uninstall unwanted programs

If you haven't used an application in more than a year, you probably never will. You can uninstall unwanted programs from Control Panel.

1 Click Start and then click Control Panel.

2 In Control Panel, click Uninstall a program.

3 Scroll through the list. Click a program name if you want to uninstall it.

4 Click Uninstall/Change.

5 Follow the prompts to uninstall the program.

 HOT TIP: Look for programs in the list that start with the name of the manufacturer of your computer, such as Acer, Hewlett-Packard or Dell.

 ALERT: Your computer may have come with programs that you don't even know about. Perform the steps above to find out.

Use Disk Cleanup

Disk Cleanup is a safe and effective way to reduce unnecessary data on your PC. With unnecessary data deleted, your PC will run faster and have more available disk space for saving files and installing programs. With Disk Cleanup you can remove temporary files, empty the Recycle Bin, remove set-up log files and remove downloaded program files, all in a single process.

1 Click Start.

2 In the Start Search dialogue box, type Disk Cleanup.

3 In the results, under Programs click Disk Cleanup Options.

4 Choose My Files Only to clean your files and nothing else. Choose Files from all users on this computer if you wish to clean additional users' files.

5 If prompted to choose a drive or partition, choose the letter of the drive that contains the operating system, this is almost always C:, but occasionally it is D:. Click OK.

6 Select the files that you want to delete. Accept the defaults if you aren't sure.

7 Click OK to start the cleaning process.

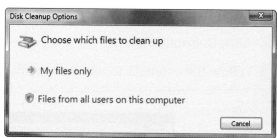

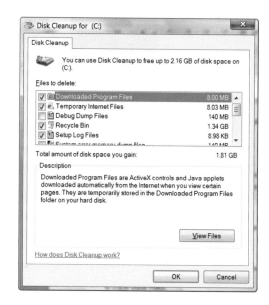

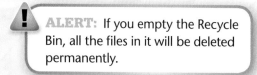

ALERT: If you empty the Recycle Bin, all the files in it will be deleted permanently.

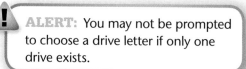

ALERT: You may not be prompted to choose a drive letter if only one drive exists.

WHAT DOES THIS MEAN?

Downloaded Program Files: Files that download automatically when you view certain webpages. They are stored temporarily in a folder on your hard disk and then accessed when and if needed.

Temporary Internet Files: These files contain copies of webpages that you've visited on your hard drive, so that you can view the pages more quickly when you visit them again.

Offline Webpages: Webpages that you've chosen to store on your computer so you can view them without being connected to the Internet. Upon connection, the data are synchronised.

Recycle Bin: Contains files that you've deleted. Files are not deleted permanently until you empty the Recycle Bin.

Setup Log Files: Files created by Windows during set-up processes.

Temporary Files: Files created and stored by programs for use by those programs. Most of these temporary files are deleted when you exit the program, but some do remain.

Thumbnails: Small icons of your pictures, videos and documents. Thumbnails will be recreated as needed, even if you delete them here.

Per user archived Windows Error Reporting: Files used for error reporting and solution checking.

System archived Windows Error Reporting: Files used for error reporting and solution checking.

Use Disk Defragmenter

A hard drive stores the files and data on your computer. When you want to access a file, the hard drive spins and data are accessed from the drive. When the data required for the file you need are all in one place, the data are accessed more quickly than if they are scattered across the hard drive in different areas. When data are scattered, they are said to be fragmented.

1 Click Start.

2 In the Start Search dialogue box, type Defrag.

3 Under Programs, select Disk Defragmenter.

4 Verify that Disk Defragmenter is configured to run on a schedule. If not, place a tick in the appropriate box.

5 To manually run Disk Defragmenter, click Defragment now.

6 Click OK.

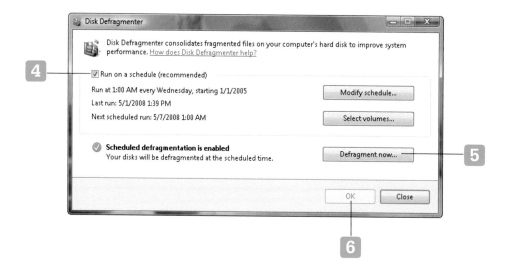

? DID YOU KNOW?

Disk Defragmenter analyses the data stored on your hard drive and consolidates files that are not stored together.

? DID YOU KNOW?

By default, Disk Defragmenter runs automatically, and on a schedule, but it is best to verify this.

Top 10 Computer Basics Problems Solved

Problem 1: A piece of hardware doesn't work

To solve this problem, you must troubleshoot the hardware problem:

1 If the hardware needs to be connected to a power source, make sure it is. You may also want to check to see whether the power source is working.

2 Insert fresh batteries, if applicable.

3 Check the connection from the device to the PC.

4 If a cable is bent, frayed or damaged, replace it.

5 Turn on the device, if applicable.

6 Open Help and Support and click Troubleshooting for more information.

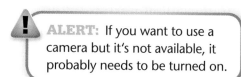

ALERT: If you want to use a camera but it's not available, it probably needs to be turned on.

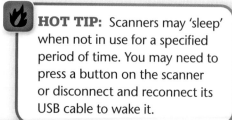

HOT TIP: Most digital cameras must be turned on and put in 'playback' mode to be recognised by Windows Vista.

HOT TIP: Scanners may 'sleep' when not in use for a specified period of time. You may need to press a button on the scanner or disconnect and reconnect its USB cable to wake it.

Problem 2: I can't find a file that I previously saved

Certain files are saved, by default, in your personal folders. Always check your Documents folder, Pictures folder and related folders. If you don't find the file there, you'll have to search for it.

1 Click Start.

2 In Vista, in the Start Search window type the name of the file.

3 Click the file to open it. There will be multiple search results.

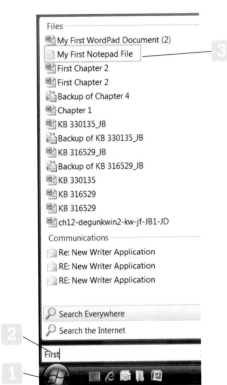

? **DID YOU KNOW?**

Windows XP does not have a Start Search window, and thus you'll have to use a different method: click Start, click Search and then use the available search tools there.

? **DID YOU KNOW?**

If you don't know any part of the name of the file, you can type a word that is included inside the file or just search for a specific type of file.

! **ALERT:** If you don't know the exact name of the file, you can type just part of the name.

Problem 3: I can't use my PC effectively because of a disability

If you find it difficult to use your PC effectively because of a disability, such as a hearing, vision or dexterity problem, Vista can help.

1 Click Start, and in the Start Search window type Ease.

2 Under Programs, click Ease of Access Center.

3 Click Get recommendations to make your computer easier to use.

4 Answer the questions as they are asked, clicking Next to move to the next screen.

5 Configure the recommended settings in the Ease of Access Center.

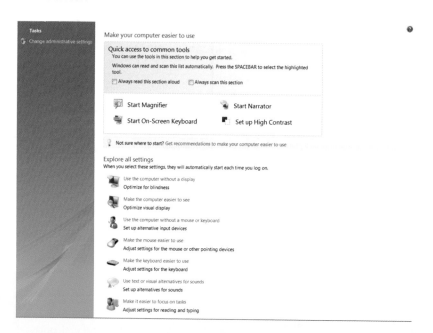

ALERT: This section applies only to Vista users.

Problem 4: I get too much junk email

There are four filtering options in Windows Mail: No automatic filtering, Low, High, and Safe List Only. These options let you choose how you will deal with spam. In Windows Mail:

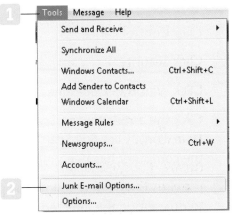

1. Click Tools.

2. Click Junk E-mail Options.

3. From the Options tab, make a selection.

4. Click the Phishing tab.

5. Select Protect my Inbox from messages with potential Phishing links. Additionally, move phishing email to the Junk E-Mail folder.

6. Click OK.

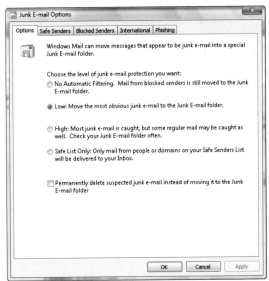

Problem 5: I suspect my computer may have a virus

Use Windows Defender to run a manual scan for viruses:

1 Click Start.

2 Click Control Panel.

3 Click Security.

 Windows Defender
Scan for spyware and other potentially unwanted software

4 Click Windows Defender.

5 Click the arrow next to Scan (not the Scan icon). Click Full Scan if you think the computer has been infected.

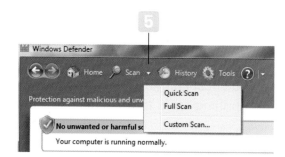

6 If a virus is detected, follow the prompts to quarantine the infected files.

7 Click the X in the top right corner to close the Windows Defender window.

 HOT TIP: Viruses often come in the form of an email attachment. Never open an attachment from someone you don't know.

 HOT TIP: You can get a virus from the Internet via a download. When you download data from the Internet make sure it comes from a trusted source, like Microsoft, Adobe or Amazon to name a few.

Problem 6: One of the pictures I've uploaded has a subject with red eye. I want to remove this from the picture

The Fix Red Eye tool lets you draw a rectangle around any eye that has a red dot in it so you can remove the red dot.

1. Open Photo Gallery.

2. Double-click a picture that you want to edit.

3. Click Fix.

4. Click Fix Red Eye.

5. Drag the mouse over the red part of the eye. When you let go, the red eye in the picture will be removed.

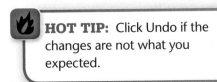 **HOT TIP:** Click Undo if the changes are not what you expected.

Problem 7: My computer doesn't do what I want it to do when I insert a blank CD, DVD movie or music CD

You can tell Vista what you want it to do when you insert or access media by changing the autoplay settings in Control Panel.

1 Click Start.

2 Click Default Programs on the Start menu.

3 Click Change AutoPlay settings.

4 Use the drop-down lists to select the program that you want to use for the media you want to play.

5 Click Save.

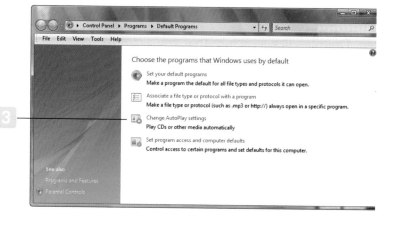

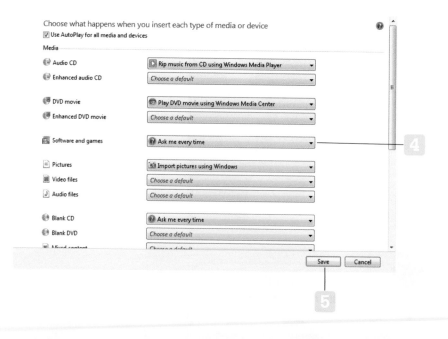

Problem 8: I've downloaded or installed software or hardware that caused a problem for the computer, and the computer now seems unstable

Run System Restore:

1. Open System Restore.

2. Click Next to accept and apply the recommended restore point.

3. Click Finish.

ALERT: If you're running System Restore on a laptop, make sure the laptop is plugged it. System Restore should never be interrupted

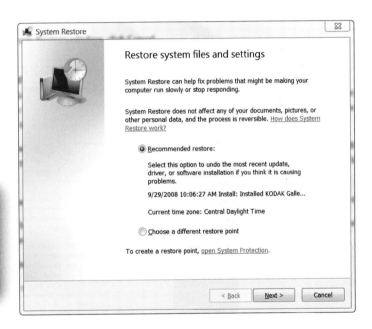

Problem 9: It takes a long time for my computer to complete the boot-up process

You may have too many programs trying to start when Windows does. You need to disable some of them from starting.

1. Click Start.

2. In the Start Search window, type System Configuration.

3. Under Programs, click System Configuration.

4. From the Startup tab, deselect third-party programs that you recognise but do not use daily.

5. Click OK.

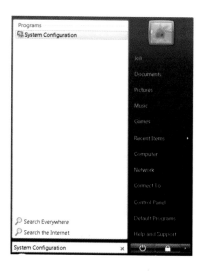

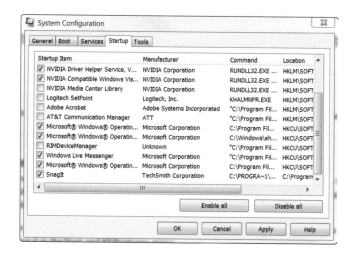

ALERT: Do not deselect anything you don't recognise or the operating system!

ALERT: You'll have to restart the computer in order to apply the changes.

Problem 10: I could connect to the Internet yesterday, but today I can't

When you have a problem connecting to your local network or to the Internet, you can often resolve the problem in the Network and Sharing Center.

 ALERT: Make sure your cable modem, router, cables and other hardware are properly connected, plugged in and turned on.

Network and Sharing Center

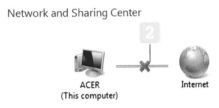

ACER
(This computer)

Internet

 Open the Network and Sharing Center.

 Click the red X.

 Not connected

 ALERT: You won't see a red X if the network is functioning properly.

 Perform the steps in the order in which they are presented.

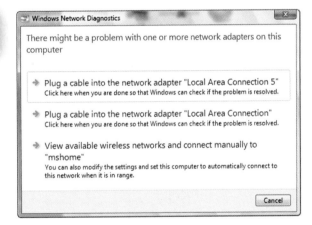

Windows Network Diagnostics

There might be a problem with one or more network adapters on this computer

➔ Plug a cable into the network adapter "Local Area Connection 5"
Click here when you are done so that Windows can check if the problem is resolved.

➔ Plug a cable into the network adapter "Local Area Connection"
Click here when you are done so that Windows can check if the problem is resolved.

➔ View available wireless networks and connect manually to "mshome"
You can also modify the settings and set this computer to automatically connect to this network when it is in range.

Cancel

 DID YOU KNOW?
Almost all of the time, performing the first step will resolve your network problem.

 ALERT: If prompted to reset your broadband or satellite connection, turn off all hardware, including the computer, and restart them in the following order: cable/satellite/DSL modem, router, computers.

 ALERT: When restarting a cable or satellite modem, remove any batteries to completely turn off the modem.